Twin

Flame

Discover the Mythology of Soul
Mates and the Twin Flame Union

*(The Secret to Unlocking Unconditional Love &
Finding Your Way Home)*

Erik Nolasco

Published By **Darby Connor**

Erik Nolasco

All Rights Reserved

Twin Flame: Discover the Mythology of Soul Mates and the Twin Flame Union (The Secret to Unlocking Unconditional Love & Finding Your Way Home)

ISBN   978-1-998038-23-7

Legal & Disclaimer

Table Of Contents

Chapter 1: History and Mythology of Twin Flames

In the start come to be your a Twin soul, owning yin and yang, masculine and female, sides of the identical coin, contrary, and however-neither entire without the possibility. When you had been created you have been in Spirit with God, Spirit-Light and Oneness. Like an atom you had been cut up into elements, but you've got been bound to the other part of you like a magnet is interested by its polar opposite.

Even regardless of the reality which you're separate, you are also collectively due to the truth you have been created to healthy collectively, twin souls, dual flames, sure collectively for now and all the time. You most effective have one twin flame who's your completeness. You may additionally have many human beings to whom you're attracted, and you may have soul buddies, however these aren't just like dual flames.

Your dual flame resonates on the same vibration of hobby as you do, and you can immediately be part of even as your paths float.

Two halves of 1 entity is best the start of the tale. After we were created, we have come to be displaced from the utter blissfulness of Being that emerge as Oneness to go back into lifestyles into the bodily global wherein we now abide. We lengthy for the religious Oneness with the Universe in which we were whole and entire, one in concord with all beings, spiritual and bodily. When we left the holiness of the Oneness, we've grow to be a bereaved and lonely soul searching for of entirety, travelling many lifetimes and journeys as we searched for each ourselves and our Twin Flame. This journey has been shared thru many souls throughout records, and I will percent only a few abbreviated sagas with you as allusions of our culminating destiny.

Throughout records there have been examples of the greatest love memories within the international, acquainted to severa us as romantic couplings or friendships which is probably deep and affectionate; the ones memories are also the mythology and records of Twin Flames. These testimonies resonate with a deep love and passion, but in addition they pass past mere physicality. They also are reminiscences of recognize and reverence, spirit beings in a physical form that have joined to finish their issuer artwork that has been planted through the Universe.

Perhaps the most familiar to those of the Judeo-Christian way of life is the story of Adam and Eve. However, I would like to start with a excellent earlier tale, the parable of Zeus and the Gods, moreover referred to as, How Humankind Became Split.

How Humankind Became Split

At the begin, people had been created within the entirety of wholeness, every person have end up half of male and half of girl. They seemed as although a notable sphere, with arms and legs for absolutely everyone. As hands and two legs have been a complete of eight limbs for anyone, this gave them energy and agility lots more than we've nowadays, with definitely legs and arms each. This amazing robustness proved to be very effective, so fantastic, that the Gods have been threatened via their electricity.

Zeus and the remaining Gods resolved that sports had been occurring too fast and there has been too much electricity in Humankind. They decided to break up the Humans into , with first-rate hands and two legs. Since the time the Whole Humans had been cut up, they were looking for their different half of of.

The Speech of Aristophanes

Plato's symposium, The Speech of Aristophanes, concludes with this notorious interpretation of Twin Flames:

'Do you preference to be absolutely one; typically day and night time time in each special's company commercial enterprise organisation? For if that is what you choice, I am prepared to soften and fuse you collectively, in order that being you shall turn out to be one, and while you stay live a commonplace lifestyles as if you had been a single man, and after your lack of existence within the global beneath but be one departed soul, rather than --I ask whether that is what you lovingly choice and whether or not or no longer you're happy to gain this?'-

There isn't always a person of them who at the same time as he heard the concept may also deny or need to not renowned that this assembly and melting into every one of a kind, this turning into one in place of , modified into the very expression of his ancient need.

And the motive is that human nature become at the start one and we were a whole, and the preference and pursuit of the whole is referred to as love.

Adam and Eve

From Adam and Eve we see the complex fable of introduction as informed in the ebook of Genesis. The first scripture regarding Humanity says that God created each male and lady:

"So God created guy in his own photograph, inside the picture of God created he him; male and lady created he them". (Gen 1: 26)

These scriptures verify they may be split into equally built Humans, in a parallel to the tale from Plato. It takes two halves, male and female personas, to make one Whole in the circle of existence. At this thing there was one (Adam), with each traits of girl and masculine. Then God cut up Adam through taking his rib (Gen. 2:21) and made Eve. This end up the Divine Split that separated Adam and Eve into separate beings. They end up whole yet again on the same time because the Twin Flames are rejoined, as said in Gen. 2:24.

"Therefore shall a person depart his father and his mom, and shall cleave unto his partner; and that they may be one flesh" (Gen 2:24)

Genesis 2:24 way that the Twin Flames have been although in reference to every other, however have no longer merged into Oneness. Twin Flame Oneness (one flesh) is an immoderate amalgamation of feeling, love, completeness, and concord with the Universe.

David and Jonathan

The tale of David and Jonathan that is recommended in 1 Samuel is an example of Twin Flames that aren't reserved to male/female couplings, however can also be equal intercourse, or occasionally brother/sister. Twin Flames are the merging of Divine Spirit and Love, moderate, vibration and resonance, now not to be confused with sexual love.

The parallel of Twin Flames becoming one, as in the first recollections, is found within the following Scripture:

"After David had completed speakme with Saul, Jonathan have become one in spirit with David, and he loved him as himself." (I Samuel 18:1)

Finding your Twin Flame entails evolving from one this is self-centered and burdened, to at least one that is in spiritual connection and right courting with the Creator.

One might probably wonder why it's far crucial for the 2 souls to turn out to be separated, but how else are we able to develop spiritually to understand our crowning glory if do no longer first undergo the loneliness and chaos of an empty soul? If we have been in no way break up aside, then how do we search for our Spiritual cause this is to advantage the Universe? It is in our aloneness that we begin to discover who we're in phrases of creativity, will, truth, and cause.

As we keep our adventure inside the exploration of self, we begin having excessive feelings of craving for our specific half of, our Twin Flame. We grieve for that which isn't however to be as we don't forget the feelings of wholeness. Sometimes we honestly cry from loneliness, no longer the squalling cry of the child who has out of area his preferred toy, but the deep heartfelt sobs of the kid who has been torn from his mom's breast and is now feels desolate and deserted.

Papatuanuku and Ranginui

These deep emotions of separation and loss are conveyed inside the legend of

Papatuanuku and Ranginui, within the Maori Creation story. Ranginui have become the sky. He and Papatuanuku have been born inside the vacancy called Te Po. They had been so in love that they held each different constantly, interconnected and embracing. Even in spite of the truth that they have got been never aside, they had numerous kids. The children grew unhappy living in the darkness and feature come to be jealous of the closeness of Ranginui and Papatuanuku. The kids conspired together and flung them aside, placing Ranginui above as moderate. This become the separation of darkness and slight (Te Ao Marama). Papatuanuku changed into stored underneath as darkness. Ranginui and Papatuanuku without surrender grieve to be collectively. Sometimes Rangi cries tears from the heavens due to the fact he misses Papa plenty. Sometimes Papa breaks herself aside like mist to try and connect to Rangi, but she cannot pretty achieve him.

Each soul grieves for the alternative, looking desperately to reunite in Oneness.

The Twin Flame in information is asking as avidly as we are to reconnect to that one with whom we can be without stop ushered into the Being of One. Once we're rejoined, our Oneness with the Universe will compel to finish the spiritual motive that conjoins us to the One Spirit this is the finishing touch of all.

Purusha and Prakriti

The literal which means of the Hindu God Ardhanarishvara is "The Lord who's half woman", a consultant title that inspires the picture of the synthesis of the lady and masculine strength of the Universe. In Sanskrit, Spirit and Matter are recognized as Purusha and Prakriti. It is thru this story that we begin to understand the motive of our Being.

Spirit relies upon Matter for manifestation. Without the concord of Matter, Spirit is unconditioned, subjective, and undifferentiated in its no-issue-ness. Matter desires Spirit for route. Without Spirit, Matter is chaotic and with out reason, a barren entity.

The Source of Purusha and Prakriti is the One, the Brahman, made from every Spirit and Matter. The elements are one and the equal substance; Matter is the materialization of Spirit and Spirit is the manifestation of Matter. Together they may be the One. It is inside the will of the One that Twin Flames are cohesive and fulfilled.

Once we are rejoined with our Twin Flame, that isn't the final undertaking for which we're charged. We have one extra very essential project. This is the last vocation for every twin flame reunited, and that is exemplified through the parable from Ancient Sumeria.

Dumuzi and Inanna

In Ancient Sumeria, the Divine Union of Dumuzi and Inanna is related to Divine Love and captivating, romantic poetry. Inanna is also called the Queen of Heaven and Earth. Inanna is aligned with the Planet Venus, whose feature is to herald romantic love. Venus also ushers in Wisdom, which can be embodied thru particular attributes in each humans.

Enki proficient Inanna with severa unique presents referred to as Mes. Through her Shepherd King Dumuzi, she took her Divine presents and prolonged them to gain the Universe. When Venus is flowing via a Twin Flame this is soul-targeted upon reuniting with the One, the Twin Flame initiates acts of kindness and willful motive to put together humanity for courting with the Spirit. These acts of motive start whilst Venus synthesizes love from a romantic dating right into a cohesive partnership and alliance that artwork together for the Divine Will. Inanna suggests us this same purpose while, after the Divine Union with Dumuzi, she/he (the Twin Flame couple) took their gadgets and increased them for the goodness of the One. When we meet and rejoin with our Twin Flame, we are capable of furthermore act upon our cause of the Will of the Divine.

Sri Aurobindo and the Mother

As we end this chapter, we are able to go to the story of Sri Aurobindo and the Mother. This twin flame duet, as Sri Aurobindo stated, are the embodiment of that have become one. They have been so bonded that they may communicate telepathically. Their reason changed into to typify the Shiva and Shakti power proper here on earth and display us an instance of twin soul issuer. The Mother sums up the connection with the intention to exist even as you're reconciled collectively together with your Twin Flame, "Without him, I exist no longer; with out me, he is unmanifest."

Chapter 2: What are Twin Flames?

Twin Flames, used interchangeably with the time period dual souls, are the alternative a part of our beings. We each have one same twin soul, that changed into connected collectively in our advent. When we had been split, we went into our separate geographical regions. We have been incarnating time and again to accumulate our desired character reviews in order to complete our spiritual growth before we can come all over again to very last contact.

Twin Flame reunification is the remaining stop bring about a dating. The most a laugh courting is the reuniting of the 2 souls into one. Twin Flame couples are uncommon to find. However, because of the wonderful instances that we're dwelling, an increasing number of couples are locating their Twin Flame. This is due to the non secular transformation and soul paintings that humans are experiencing. Our information of the soul and spirit are evolving thru openness and education. What in advance than took lifetimes to analyze and revel in, humans now are receiving and responding inner a few months or years. This is an awesome acceleration this is propelling at some point of the planet and Universe.

Twin Flames have a reason. Their reuniting is a Cosmic occasion, for a religious motive. Through their union, revolutionary strength is released for his or her religious assignment. Many Twins use their energy to help the planet or guide humanity towards the Consciousness of One.

Twin Flames need to be spiritually organized for the union or they may now not be capable of abide the intensity of the relationship. In a Twin Flame dating, there will now not anything amongst you. There might be no secrets and techniques, no hidden knowledge, no past intrusions into this life. Your threat of meeting your Twin Flame is surely relying on your spiritual boom. If your soul is cleansed of divisiveness, when you have cleared your emotional hurdles, when you have removed the baggage from your beyond lives, you may be organized for your Twin Flame. If you have not advanced your soul art work, this can be a damaged sadness for you.

When Twin Flames reunify, each of the souls have an quickening of religious increase and transformative reanimation of their cause. They absorb short the esoteric facts

intertwined in a popularity that would see others around them, but is so whole they're a separate entity to themselves. They are One, but complete selves additionally. When they in the long run reunite, it's miles like coming domestic for the primary time and the final time.

Chapter 3: Karmic Soul Partnerships and False Twins

Karmic Soul Partnerships

A Karmic courting is a deep bond among people to stability the Karma on your existence. A Karmic courting is neither your Soul Mate nor your Twin Flame.

Some humans enter our lives and touch it so intensely that they leave lasting footprints on our coronary coronary heart and soul. Such someone is your Karmic Soul Mate.

The Karmic Soul Mate enters your existence to teach you a life lesson or to manual your inner path. Sometimes they're there to help you in a specific religious assignment. You will sense a completely unique closeness with this individual. You can be attracted like a nail to a magnet. The accurate or lousy energy of this dating is related for your past existence with this man or woman, due to the fact the interconnection and Karmic electricity is relative to the previous contact.

The mystery of the conjunction is to balance the karma.

It may be there are many arguments and anger from this Karmic relationship. There can be masses unfinished commercial enterprise. If you do not heal the rifts among you and your Karmic Soul Mate, your emotions and soul might be pressured and chaotic. You might also even enjoy stuck with out a go together with the flow, or chi, on your lifestyles. Here are some processes to pick out a Karmic on your life:

● A bond of appeal so sturdy you cannot manipulate your thoughts about them.

● A deep preference for them to love you.

● You often argue, combat and live in disharmony.

● You may furthermore allow their horrible behavior and addictions.

- You have tips for your relationships with friends, or controlling behaviors.

- You experience codependent on them, looking their popularity of your selections.

- You deliver up the beyond for your arguments and fights, in no way resolving problems.

- The other desires to direct your existence in place of specializing of their lifestyles.

- The dating and all its drama makes you experience depressed and doubt yourself.

This dating can be toxic because the possibility man or woman can be maintaining your employer to use your home for themselves. You want to reduce your dating off as it's far very difficult to be happy in a Karmic dating. The humans use each one-of-a-kind up till there may be no energy left from which to increase and assemble.

Instead of being love, that is infatuation and being in love with love. Often, it is the relationship (identifying your self as being "taken") and belonging this is more important than the alternative individual.

The only manner to make a Karmic courting paintings is to be in balance via resolving all of the beyond issues of anger and mistrust. If you do no longer do the recuperation paintings, you may repeat this dating time and again with new companions, however the equal behaviors.

To remedy the Karmic disharmony, we want to prevent the sample and feelings thru studying the lesson that is repeated. We frequently do not understand the underlying pattern till we have a study the lesson. When we examine what is needed and practice the new behavior, the pattern ends.

"When the scholar is prepared, the instructor will appear" is all about Karmic relationships.

False Twins

Sometimes we're so needy for a dating that we mistakenly emerge as aware about someone as a twin that isn't always one. When we're in a happy relationship, we want the massive other to be our Twin. We even occasionally bask in "magical wondering" to motive them to grow to be, in our myth global, the Twin we want them to be. We will stretch the truth until we're unaware of our real relationship, or perhaps to our non-public sadness. We keep close to like greedy youngsters at the topics which is probably working so we do no longer have test the unsightly thorn in our foot. When the connection and goodness has died, every body spherical us has discovered the negativity in our electricity and thoughts-set, but we maintain the phantasm until it hurts loads we're able to not undergo the ache.

With our karma we formulate our lifestyles plan. We have the freedom to select to stroll away from a toxic courting. Just due to the reality we as quickly as idea that it become actual does not advocate that is how lifestyles must be. We can alternate, apprehend the connection wishes to trade, or we will abandon this revel in for the mastering we've were given determined out and circulate to the subsequent improvement.

From the immediate we're separated from our Twin Flame, we are assured that we are capable of be joined collectively another time.

Our loneliness makes us susceptible. Our vulnerability is what makes us open to like. We also can collect a fact that offers us all our dreams, but it is high-quality a production. It is pretty on the outdoor but hollow under.

Do your soul work. Search on your religious awakening. Don't settle for someone or a few element this is artificial even as you can hold in touch with herbal Essence of Life. Wait on your Twin Flame in desire to constructing your personal model. Continue on foot closer to the Light and you may discover yourself subsequently within the Light of Love United.

Chapter 4: What are Soulmates?

Soulmates are the own family that changed into created with us from the begin. According to mythology, whilst the soul is created, or born from the One, it's miles built in a set. The souls that have been constructed in this equal totality are our soulmates, our comparable beings, however not our twins, and no longer our existence partners. When the ones souls are split, that makes our Twin Flame.

A soulmate is near in mind and reviews at the soul level, now not continually the physical degree. You may be related at a while, like sisters or brothers, you may be extremely good pals in a one-of-a-kind lifetime, you'll be instructor and pupil, or figure and child.

Soulmates assist us broaden, boom, and expend karma. Our conversations are deeply rooted in private boom and spiritual issuer. There is a deep shared love and problem for spiritual yearnings, not superficial topics of earthly frivolities.

From Theosophy by using manner of Edgar Cayce

God created souls which have been androgynous, in addition male and female. These souls break up into separate beings and genders, now not in a single accord. When they separated from God they incurred Karma. Now they are in search of for each unique to head once more to God, however first they need to clean all karmic interference. Only then can they reunite and move back to the Ultimate One.

Aspects of a Soulmate Relationship

• Equality in enchantment

• Very deep feelings for each other

• Calm inside the presence from inside and without

• Trust a number of the two

- Connectiveness on the onset

- Not judgmental, terrible or critical

- Unconditional positive regard

- Always sharing

- Make you the priority

- Gentle in all situations towards you

- Non-restrictive

This dating may be one among happiness and contentment. This is the character you could sit beside, in no way say a word, however realize right away the spirit of the alternative individual.

Your soulmate will no longer be your lover nor your lifestyles accomplice. Your soulmate will not be simply one man or woman, it's going to likely be many people sooner or later of all your lifetimes. You will no longer constantly be in perfect alignment in all subjects, but you may mirror each other.

Your soulmate will mission you on your complacency. Your soulmate will strive to help you achieve your private super. Your soulmate will assist you reap a higher diploma of soul interest. Once you've got were given reached the training your soulmate shares, you can bodily separate.

Chapter 5: How to inform the Difference Between Twin Flames and Soulmates

Sometimes the terms Soulmate and Twin Flames are used interchangeably, but they may be now not one and the same.

Here are some of the variations so that you can recognize the versions:

A soulmate can occur usually in masses of lifetimes for you

A Twin Flame is the opportunity half of of your soul

A soulmate also can cause trauma whilst exploring feelings and emotions

A Twin Flame has already resolved all Karmic troubles so there can be a deep feeling of peace

Sex with a soulmate may be pleasing and a laugh

Sex with a Twin Flame can be mind blowing due to the fact the relationship is so deep and wondrous

When soulmates separate, there can be anxiety or worry

When Twin Flames separate, there is probably peace and emotions of agree with

A soulmate relationship is ready non secular increase, so it's far in no way painless

A Twin Flame courting is always painless, and looks as if a homecoming of pleasure

Chapter 6: Synchronicity and Signs you can have met your Twin Flame or Spiritual Partner

Synchronicity

Synchronicity is based totally at the foundational principle that each one activities have which means and now not anything is twist of destiny. Have you ever revel in an prevalence that became so now not likely it left you in surprise? Let me provide you with an instance.

My sister turned into the usage of to her scientific physician's place of work, twenty seven miles from her domestic. As she drove down a very busy dual carriageway, she observed a package deal fly out of a shipping vehicle. She stopped at the aspect of the dual carriageway, at the shoulder, and walked decrease lower returned to the bundle to drop it at the nearest parcel service place of business. When she picked up the package deal, she glanced on the zip code and become surprised to see it became her private zip code. She appeared closer at the tiny kind at the label and the bundle deal have come to be addressed to her husband!

It turn out to be a remedy he needed at once and he grow to be at domestic searching forward to the delivery. Was this an insignificant twist of destiny that she happened to look the package deal fall in a place she hardly ever traveled? I assume now not!

This is an instance of the workings of Synchronicity.

Our lives are whole of sports which can be out of our manage, but one random occasion, one blink, and lifestyles modifications. The Butterfly Effect or the Domino Effect, one occurring across the world influences our small lives in momentous techniques.

Have you seen examples of Synchronicity on your life? Johnny Depp has. He become accompanying a chum to an audition for a issue in a movie. He wasn't even an actor however he modified into stable for the detail. He did not actually have a take a look at! That have turn out to be synchronicity.

Chaos idea is the understanding that the sector is entire of random events, however that one small alternate has rippling results, additionally referred to as The Butterfly Effect.

Have you seen this seem on your existence? Have you placed your self taking a unique path or going a completely unique way and having a "risk stumble upon" that modified your existence?

I did. I changed into going to a meeting at a place I had in no way been, on a day I in no manner traveled, to speak with humans I definitely have never met. I in no manner went again to that location. But at that meeting, on that day, I decided my Twin Flame. The date? 1.1

Any distortion of the Divine Fabric, no matter how small, provokes lifestyles changing outcomes. Everything is associated, the past, the winning and the destiny are all a unifying circle.

We are all related through our personal Source.

Our cognizance is installation thru vicinity and time. What we see proper right here, in the present, is most effective a shadow of the actual international of Oneness. There is a international past this barrier we call "existence as we apprehend it", a worldwide of interconnectedness.

What you be aware and revel in is in element non-public to you. It is your interpretation thru the filters of your recognition. Didn't you have a look at that when your religious awakening the area have become brighter, bolder, with more flavors? The worldwide has typically been this colorful, however your interpretations and perceptions changed.

Synchronicity is channeling the power you emit into an an recognition of existence. When your religious vibration fits your goals that you are looking for for you can gather your dreams. The Universe will discover a manner. The extra deeply you connect to the Universe, the more synchronicities you could locate, due to the fact your ideals will channel the synchronicities in a powerful manner to reflect your dreams.

Every step you're taking and each breath you are making affects the lives of others.

eleven Signs you have got met your Twin Flame or Spiritual Partner

Here are a few symptoms to look for to confirm you've got got were given met your Twin Flame or Spiritual Partner:

1. You revel in a deep, non secular connection with this character not like you

have ever skilled earlier than. You revel in like you have were given walked onto a better aircraft. You feel lighter, brighter and further in music along side your religious self. You experience within the Presence of the Source even as you're with them.

2. You have had visions or goals of them appearing and reappearing on your existence. You have commonly felt their presence, even supposing they had been now not physical gift. You furthermore feels waves of splendid strength flowing thru you, listen a track play and realise it triggers a few issue internal, different synchronicities like noticing 11:11 at the clock at ordinary happenings. You have occurrences of outdoor influences you feature to spirits or angels.

3. You recognize which you have a beyond with this individual, even if you've only honestly met. You can endure in thoughts statistics of your past lives collectively as though they had been the day prior to this.

The other person triggers powerful feelings due to your excessive connection.

"Your coronary coronary coronary heart and my coronary coronary heart are very, very vintage buddies." Hafiz

4. You and your Twin Flame percent the identical soul, however have differing personalities. You are not codependent, however you have similar likes in crucial matters. You are not twins like same twins, however greater like fraternal twins. You can express your individuality and complement each other. Each of you is one half of of of the equation, the yin/yang to every one of a kind.

5. You have this form of deep psychic interest of each different that you can experience if a few aspect is wrong. You be a part of in a telepathic way that is going past mere verbal conversation, notwithstanding the truth which you often cease every awesome's sentences and

understand what the alternative is saying earlier than the phrases are spoken aloud. Their happiness, specific fortune, fulfillment and properly-being are paramount to you. You positioned their dreams earlier than your private.

6. When they may be unwell, tired, worn-out, you can experience the strength seeping out of you. You echo their traumas and hurts.

7. You supply out the first-rate in them and similarly they in you. You each feed each other first rate religious power in order that your synergy is shape of a combustion of passion, creativity and strength all wrapped into one cohesive form.

eight. Despite the hardships, you each evolve and make the sector a higher vicinity. You navigate the Earthly realms so you can journey the spiritual planes.

9. You bodily hurt even as you are apart. Your soul feels empty without their

presence, regardless of the reality that you are whole.

10. You percentage unconditional love.

11. You met your companion at the same time as and wherein you least expected.

Chapter 7: What is a Spiritual Awakening and Why Do I Need One?

What is a Spiritual Awakening?

A spiritual awakening is as tons a physical phenomenon as it's miles a intellectual and emotional experience. Be organized for all three of those manifestations while you're present gadget religious awakening.

A non secular awakening is whilst one has end up privy to themselves in a hyper touchy knowing. The character will have a deeper awareness in their bodily feelings and surroundings. The man or woman may have a deeper records in their life traumas and pain. The character will see life in some other manner, as a adventure of instructions and learnings in choice to a "hard avenue to tour." The person can have a understanding and peace within themselves this is foundational.

The man or woman who's gift technique a non secular awakening will unexpectedly apprehend who they're and what their cause or project is to assist the Universe. The wakened individual will accept the happenings in their studies as activities, instead of centered arrows of harm and negativity.

A religious awakening can be difficult for their perception device, as an awakening will trade one's perspective on the whole lot round them. They will see themselves and the place in a specific way.

At first the awakening may be stunning because it calls for observance of the real self, and every now and then that may be pretty ugly. An awakening brings to the floor one's real region inside the Universe. Responsibilities will emerge of which the individual have grow to be unaware. The individual will understand they've a purpose and a reason to be. It may take years for the character to go back at peace inner themselves.

A non secular awakening can arise in a life transition, spontaneously, or at the lack of existence of a loved one. A close to dying experience often triggers a spiritual awakening and feel of popularity. The religious awakening activates self focus and actions one out of the autopilot mode and into simply living and revel in existence at its center.

Once you embark on the non secular awakening it will be like a mist has cleared earlier than you. Where formerly you observed most effective a glimmer of fact, now you can see pristinely. You will become impatient with shallow humans as you end up greater in contact along side your soul. You will look all over again at your previous existence and realize how masses come to be wasted on your selfishness. You will advantage the capability to position self apart and flow toward the One who sustains.

One part of the religious awakening is the affirmation of the ripple effect. What you do makes an effect on the rest of the Universe, even if you do no longer see the effect or acknowledge it. You have fee and your expression of self adjustments the lives and spiritual being of different spiritual beings. You can exchange your sphere of have an impact on into truely one among exceptional power and reflectiveness, and as you do, you can see others change with you. Your transition will create the domino effect for the ones surrounding you.

Purposes for a Spiritual Awakening

1. To find out who you clearly are, the non secular self, the actual inner being this is related to the Universe.

2. To increase you better on a spiritual plane.

three. To end up self-conscious.

4. To discover self as regards to the Universe, and to enlarge from this exploration.

5. To learn how to love self and take transport of self in which you are.

6. To discover ways to love others and receive others wherein they will be.

7. To discover your spiritual objects that you may use to help the Earth.

8. To find out your calling in existence.

nine. To spiritually hook up with the Source, the people, the planet, and all beings.

10. To understand that every one topics are associated.

eleven. To open you to new spiritual understandings.

12. To decorate your vibrations.

The 5 Stages of a Spiritual Awakening

A religious awakening has five levels, each one is unique and precise for anyone. Your time frame is your timetable, no longer a person else's. This isn't a race or a opposition, it's far the fruits of your being. Savor it.

There are 5 main tiers in a non secular awakening, numbered from 1-5. Stage zero is the inactive pre-awakening stage.

Stage 0

At Stage 0 there may be no non-public hobby the least bit. The individual is occupying the body but non secular is a shell this is empty. It can take many reports of analyzing earlier than a person can start the primary stage of non secular awakening. Some humans must go through many painful studies earlier than they understand the emptiness in their soul. Other humans are born with an antique soul that instinctively is aware of wherein they're in their spiritual cognizance of the Universe and Self. A non secular awakening will display up, however not always when it's far predicted.

Stage 1

A spiritual awakening has an impetus, both a purpose or a spontaneous occasion. A cause can be a near loss of life occasion, a stressful going on, a prolonged infection, even an incarceration. Whatever spontaneous occasion that reasons someone to forestall and mirror on one's because of this that inside the international, that is the quickening of a religious awakening. The trigger will the catalyst to start the spiritual global arising. The attention of the non secular, in area of the physical, may be overwhelming. The religious awakening starts offevolved offevolved slowly via the incitement of a stimulus, from time to time an super occasion, but simply as likely a worrying loss.

Stage 2

Response, normally surprise and chaos. The start of the religious awakening can be as chaotic as an surprising death. There may be confusion, physical signs and symptoms and symptoms, overwhelming ache and grief, anger, then responds to the impetus. At this degree the person will begin to query their religious beginnings. If they may be already spiritually grounded, they'll try to dig deeper into the meanings and understandings of their teachings. If they have got in no manner earlier than been non secular, they may be exploring all kinds and manifestations of the faith adventure. This is a time of deep meditated picture and thinking of self and God, or the One, or the Source. Awareness has been spurred and now the exploration of the soul begins.

Stage 3

Chakras open and the surge of vibrations are felt. As power hums thru the 7 chakras, there is probably bodily signs and symptoms and signs and symptoms and highbrow symptoms and signs. Sometimes human beings suppose they are getting ill or going crazy. Stage 3 may be the hardest stage due to the fact all degrees of the character are affected, the bodily, the emotional, the religious, the highbrow, or maybe the energy tiers. In Stage three, the continuing flux of recent styles and emotions, even the hole of feelings will take a toll. It might be very tough and chaotic. Nothing can be taken as a proper because all the antique is lengthy beyond and the modern is rising.

Stage 3 is just like the formation of a butterfly. The vintage shell must be shed in advance than the ultra-modern soul can emerge. Breaking out of the vintage shell is uncomfortable and you are aware of wings, but they're moist and want to dry. You ought to rest severa times to allow all of your modifications to coalesce.

Sometimes the intellectual and emotional symptoms and signs and signs are overwhelming and you could need to are looking for a trusted counselor for assist. There is nothing incorrect with requesting assist, it's miles part of the learning. Awareness progresses due to the fact the chakras are opened, bringing sensations, thoughts, and emotions which can sense like confusion.

Stage four

Now you may begin to heal. Stage 4 can be a treatment after the chaos and modifications instigated in Stage 3. In Stage four, the important thing phrase is popularity. You will discover ways to take shipping of who you are, your beyond life, your reviews without a biased view, and recognition of lifestyles as a sequence of ongoing occasions in place of a bitter tablet to swallow. You will lose all anger, harm, bitterness and negativity as you permit your self to be fed on through God, the One or the Source of the Universe. The emotions of oppression you've got were given were given can be lengthy long long past. You will understand the existing of Life is satisfactory a brief gift, that this existence is only a vapor. You will begin to yearn for Oneness in this type of manner that leaving this brief us of a isn't always a painful idea. You will interest on giving and sharing and supporting, all your non secular objects will come to the leading edge of your lifestyles and being. Self-recognition advances due to the fact the recuperation device gentles the soul.

Stage 5

Spiritual awakening is whole. In Stage 5, the person is now self aware and the non secular awakening has introduced peace. This is a snug degree as you're happier with self and extra satisfied to your non-public relationships. It is a remedy to understand you are not the middle of the Universe, however you do have a motive within the

Universe. It is exciting to recognize that you do not ought to manipulate the arena and everything in it. Knowing which you are one with the Universe and associated with all things, associated with all subjects gives you a basis and place. Now you have got an anchor of being. The religious awakening is entire however the studying has definitely started. There is probably many new commands to be observed out however they may not trigger feelings of fright, anxiousness, or loss of self assurance. You will find popularity in all topics, expertise you're part of the method, no longer a cause of sick-will or irritated gods.

Chapter 8: The Law of Attraction

Steps to Letting the Universe Help discover your Twin Flame

Everyone has the choice to find their Twin Flame, their one that makes them One. Sometimes we meet a pair that virtually seem to have been created, one for the other. Other instances we meet a person single and pay attention them say, "When will I discover the One supposed for me?" It takes attempt to are looking for and discover your Twin Flame.

Here are seven movements you can take to make use of the law of attraction in an effective way.

1. Be honest. Know who you're earlier than trying to find your Twin Flame. Be honest with every person you meet, however maximum mainly, with your self. When you're equipped to just accept your self along side your flaws and graces, at the same time as you are organized to forgive

yourself your errors so you can forgive others, whilst you're in harmony with the universe and your very very personal soul, then you definitely definately definately are geared up to offer of your self to someone else. If you aren't entire you can't percentage an entire self collectively together together with your soul mate. You may be searching alternatively for a person who is needy like your self, and will multiply your shortcomings in area of building for your strengths.

2. Be prepared for a relationship. Once you realise your entire self very well, then it's time to look for your Twin Flame. The Law of Attraction is predicated upon on how badly you need want to get up. If you are equipped, the Universe will find out a way to make it seem.

three. Be observant. Many soulmates are literally the replicate picture of the alternative, both on the outside with the identical hair coloration, pores and pores and skin tone, family historical past, or bodily build, or their indoors with the identical humorousness, likes, mannerisms and chemistry so that they appear to in form together. Look for a person with the identical likes as you.

four. Focus to your venture. The Universe is working to make your courting rise up and in case you need to reconnect together together along with your Twin Flame. Don't fall into impatience or negativity. Work to growth your attention in order that you'll be conscious and prepared while you come together. Make your self look for the solution as an alternative growing your anxieties approximately your development.

five. Be alert to lifestyles. Live each 2d, cherishing what you've got had been given. Be unfastened to love and snigger. Believe. Allow synchronicity to take place.

6. Be affected person and expect the regulation of enchantment to rise up. The

Universe is unfolding because it have to. Allow yourself time to regulate to the spirit's steerage.

7. Be although. Do no longer speak your undertakings and wishes along side your friends. Do not tell them you are prepared on your soulmate. This is for you and you by myself. If you tell outsiders, they will distract with questions and remarks. You want this time to pay hobby to your openness and recognition, on your religious guidance and energy.

Chapter 9: The Awakening due to the fact the Portal to Your Twin Flame

...and proper away they understand the opportunity 1/2 of themselves at the back of the eyes of each different... The eyes had been rightly referred to as "the house home windows of the soul." Even their voices are acquainted to each specific's ears, like a remembered chord of track...Know, consequently, that from the greater silence I shall go back . . . .Forget no longer that I shall come decrease returned to you . . . . A little on the equal time as, a 2d of rest upon the wind, and each other lady shall undergo me. ~ Kahlil Gibran

As you have got completed your religious awakening, you're now ready to are attempting to find your Twin Flame. You can be in an heightened enjoy of perceptions, your psychic and soul vibrations are enormously attuned. Any disharmony is proper away felt and also you wince with the pain of it.

When you connect to your Twin Flame, you could open the channels of power in a way you've got got in no manner felt. You will revel in mental and physical sensations which is probably unknown to you. This strength is transcendent and connects to the Source, your Twin Flame, and your soulmates. It emanates Divine Love thru all dimensions, not restrained to space, time, or rely.

Once you have reunified along with your Twin Flame, the connection nice grows. What started out out with a experience or memory, a familiarity of inclusiveness, is now developing telepathically. Even though you have got commonly been one a part of the alternative, there has been the emptiness of the soul at the same time as you waited to reunite.

Language is that this form of stifling custom. Language limits the intensity of conversation just so we do now not say what we endorse and we do now not advise what we're saying. How blessed we are to have the capability talk without terms to our Twin Flame and empathically realise their feelings and emotions. We now proportion the common dimensions of emotional, physical, and intellectual states of being.

The most important connection to hold in thoughts is to remain spiritually focused and growing, so you are grounded inside the One. You have to preserve to prayer and reflect, meditate and determine your spiritual gifts and energies. The reunification of your Twin Souls connects you right away to God. You will experience the presence of the Source in all of your moves. You might be blessed by the usage of manner of the One to fulfill your religious mission.

Giving again what you have got were given received in love and mild is paramount to a wholesome religious dating with God and collectively together with your Twin Spirit. Remember that it is all about learning the lessons and centering with the One.

Chapter 10: Inspiration - True Twin Flame Reunion Testimonials and Examples in our Modern Age

Contemporary Twin Flame Couples

Twin Flames are unusual to stand up. It takes many lifetimes and masses sacred artwork in advance than Twin Flames can be reunited. Most Twin Flames spend time aside in separate incarnations, doing their soul paintings in instruction for that final reunifying very last touch.

Here on Planet Earth, there are lots of interruptions that get inside the way of finding your Twin Flame. You might also stumble upon a False Flame. You would possibly meet plenty of your soulmates, however to be within the equal place and the same realm on the equal time is uncommon. You can be married already to the wrong character. You may be married on your soulmate but discover your Twin Flame. Your Twin Flame may be patiently geared up in case you want to give up a finished gaining knowledge of but you have not learned to permit pass.

This is why we find out so few documentations and memories of Twin Flame couples. By observance we're able to suspect and deduct that the ones listed underneath are Twin Flames. Some half of of of self-recognized and function web web sites. Without their observed out permission I can not consist of their testimonies in my e-book. I even have protected some hyperlinks to Twin Flame testimonials so you can observe for your self their spiritual adventure that delivered them collectively.

Some of the modern-day dual flames are Richard and Karen Carpenter, the brother and sister developing a track duo from the 1970's. Richard and Karen every said their connectedness.

John Lennon and Yoko Ono labored tirelessly as One to promote peace and records for this worldwide. Their son, Julian Lennon, continues their paintings nowadays within the .White Feather Foundationof the feather:

"Dad as quickly as said to me that want to he pass away, if there has been some manner of letting me apprehend he changed into going to be properly enough – that we had been all going to be right enough – the message may want to come to me within the shape of a white feather. Then something occurred to me approximately ten years inside the past as soon as I end up on excursion in Australia. I even have turn out to be furnished with a white feather with the beneficial useful resource of an Aboriginal tribal elder, which clearly took my breath away. One factor for fantastic is that the white feather has constantly represented peace to me. Everywhere we look there may be disclosure, revelation and awakening!

Hollywood celebrities which might be Twin Flame couples embody:

•Sarah Jessica Parker and Matthew Broderick

•Portia de Rossi and Ellen DeGeneres

•Danny Devito and Rhea Perlman

•Brad Pitt and Angelina Jolie

•Elizabeth and Robert Barrett Browning

•Marie and Pierre Curie

•James Watson and Francis Crick

•Clark Gable and Carole Lombard

•Jeanette MacDonald and Nelson Eddy

•Goldie Hawn and Kurt Russell

•Prince Charles and Camilla

•Oprah Winfrey and Steadman Graham

•Elizabeth Taylor and Richard Burton

- Johnny Cash and June Carter Cash

- Katherine Hepburn and Spencer Tracy

- Sri Aurobindo and the Mother

- Jada Pinkett Smith and Will Smith

- The Queen of England and Prince Phillip

- Elizabeth Clare & Mark Prophet

Chapter 11: Nobody stated it have become going to be clean

A Twin Flame Relationship is not clean and can't be as compared to each distinct earthly relationship. Especially while every twins have wounds to heal, issues to remedy and come to be entire.

One of the versions is that no twin will ever keep a grudge. No depend quantity what is stated or done. A Twin Flame Relationship has come into your lifestyles to heal you, make you entire and display you which you are unconditional love.

Always bear in mind that it is a journey and now not a bus prevent. You are in this adventure collectively so you can grow to be whole as an man or woman, absolutely to go back collectively as a strength couple after your separation segment.

Nothing can ever separate you because of the fact you're one soul. Your twin is normally with you, whether or not or not there can be communication or not. Your twin is aware of the difficult paintings you're putting in to become complete. Your dual feels your electricity at the same time as you battle, but additionally on the identical time as you're thriving. Your dual is your replicate and going through the same valleys and heights as you're.

Sending your twin your strength and physical touch in 5D will purpose them to revel in you even extra, understanding which you are constantly proper right here.

Your dual is getting geared up in your effective physical union as a super deal as you're.

Ready to constructing empires with you.

It's now not about you

A Twin Flame courting is not approximately you or the opposite. It is about the better reason of you coming collectively in union.

Ego, paradigms and negativity is conquer in a Twin Flame dating because of the reality you both cause increase in each one among a type.

You and your TF want to clear all of the bullshit from your beyond and past lives to return lower lower back easy on this life time, do the painful inner art work and eventually come together.

You will mechanically apprehend while it's miles a TFR because you're dealing with your internal demons every day as long as there are unresolved problems inner you. Your twin will in no manner go away you even in case you aren't bodily collectively.

In a Twin Flame dating there is high-quality unconditional love. Your moderate shines all through the complete universe.

The Purpose of Twin Flames

It isn't always the motive of Twin Flames to make life smooth for each fantastic.

66

Twin Flames are right right here to challenge each different to dive deep into their being, clean all of the lousy leftovers from the past and past lives.

They come collectively to deliver interest, to be an perception for others and to raise the collective popularity via being the leaders and function fashions.

They are following their cause with the resource of showing their increase in interest and via combining their powers to assemble empires collectively.

Their slight shines thru every guy or girls.

The Twin Flame Journey is difficult, disturbing sometimes, painful. But on their adventure, they rather grow together and for my part. They display the collective their unconditional love for themselves, every different and the Universe.

Their journey can't be in comparison to another earthly definition of dating.

Twin Flames are one soul in physical our bodies, going through immoderate reviews and durations of incredible struggling, simply to upward push together like a Phoenix, united beneath the being involved, loving and protective wings of the Universe.

The Search in your Twin Flame

Searching to your Twin Flame is an illusion, in truth as trying to find happiness is.

A Twin Flame courting isn't a secular dating, it's miles a journey to come to be one soul all over again.

You can't find out your Twin Flame truly due to the truth you test about Twin Flames. The longing that you is probably a Twin Flame makes your private journey to become complete on this lifestyles no longer possible.

Twin Flames discover each other with out understanding about what Twin Flames are or that some issue like that even exists. It is on their adventure to recognition that they expand in focus and end up open for such things as Twin flames, movie star seeds, soul journey, Gaia.

Whether you are a Twin Flame or now not is beside the point for your existence's adventure because of the truth your adventure is set becoming whole once more, becoming your real Self another time, talking your internal reality, know-how that you are one with the whole lot.

The connection that Twin Flames revel in for every special and amongst them is the same connection that every person else is capable of revel in for and to their non-public Self.

Twin Flames are one soul in one-of-a-kind physical our bodies. Which method that everybody and the whole lot that has a soul moreover has all of the possibilities inside them to revel in the same connectedness and wholeness for themselves as Twin Flames for every one-of-a-kind.

The distinction is that Twin Flames are on a venture on this lifetime to bring recognition, be the leaders and lift the collective recognition. They are here to assist the ascension, whether or not or no longer they like it or not, whether or not or not they're geared up or no longer. They is probably prepared for this adventure as recognition rises internal them.

A Twin Flame relationship is not a romantic relationship. At least, not only. Twins are letting flow of their very non-public ego and expectations. They go away the 3-D truth matrix to ascend into 5D and past. Yes, they create empires in three-D and they accomplish that via facts their limitless potential in better dimensions, and consequently being an instance for every man or women and every soul within the universe.

You cannot choose to be a Twin Flame. You each are or not. And now not being a Twin Flame does not make you any a lot lots much less. You are one soul on your life's adventure and your education is probably comparable: become complete, understand which you are sufficient, go beyond your ego, make a contribution to humanity.

The romantic phantasm that Twin Flames are a few detail specific comes from the egoic mind. Twin Flames are not extra or much less specific than every other soul inside the universe. Just their assignment on this lifetime is outstanding.

Being a Twin Flame is not a career. It is a calling. A very silent calling as a way to spread itself as your recognition rises.

Chapter 12: False Twin?

There is this brilliant misconception: the concept of False Twins.

There are not any fake twins. And there aren't as many dual flames available as you would possibly want to anticipate. In fact, probabilities are greater which you are NOT a dual flame. Does that change a few issue? No. The journey remains the same.

Twin Flames do not have some thing to do with the romantic idea of a relationship this is rooted to your egoic mind. If your soul did no longer decide to incarnate in two super our our bodies, you're NO Twin Flame. Sorry, however that's the blatant fact.

This technique that the journey to your actual self isn't reliant on every person else however you.

People come up with the query of False Twins to decide whether or no longer or now not they are capable of invest their strength into the connection. Understand that this concept is rooted in ego.

It isn't always about the relationship for Twin Flames. It is all about their purpose. Their reason is more than themselves. The adventure to their inner reality and turning into their true selves is a prerequisite for their adventure, no longer the romantic courting idea.

The Power of Detachment

A lot of people are emotionally linked to matters, occasions, locations, human beings, goals, and outcomes. And when it is time to extend and get to the subsequent level of their lives, those attachments maintain them caught wherein they may be. For them, it is virtually too tough to permit bypass of what no longer serves them.

Being emotionally attached to something or someone manner which you make an outdoor issue more vital than you private true self. When you are related to 3 detail that not serves you, you ship out a completely clean signal that you are not geared up (however?) to move on in existence.

Life is all about growth. Success simplest comes from growth. And boom best comes from the painful experience of detaching your self from any outdoor difficulty. And this is relevant to all areas of your life: Family, Relationship, Business, Job, Spirituality, ...

In order to create the following degree of your existence you want to permit circulate of your past. If you want to create a better dating or marriage to your existence, you want to allow pass of all your beliefs, paradigms and egotistic behaviour that killed your past relationships.

For your formidable desires to advantage, you need to detach out of your past errors, highbrow blocks and actually your beyond YOU as well. Because what were given you to in that you're right now gained't get you any in addition.

You need to crack & update previous paradigms, weigh down your highbrow blocks, tame your ego & mind in advance than you are geared up to write down a new financial ruin of your monetary smash. A lot of people do not forget detaching or letting burst off any expectancies to be similar to giving up. That is not right. On the other, please preserve in mind that at the same time as you detach from any expected final results or purpose, you're starting as a good buy as opportunities which is probably a tremendous deal huge and higher than you can have ever imagined.

When setting dreams, humans commonly tend to set desires from their thoughts-set of possibility. Every individual is living of their very non-public consolation region and „box". That's why thinking outside the sphere is so tough for plenty. When you're placing your goals, you purpose for some aspect this is possible from your notion. At maximum, you're bending your consolation sector a hint. If, then, you're insisting in this very final consequences, you're restricting your self and depriving your self of the loads big and higher opportunities which is probably to be had to you. And the extraordinary trouble is that you aren't even aware about the more opportunities due to the fact you in truth cannot keep near the abundance of the universe.

Again, this applies to all regions of your life. You must detach from your spouse, your agency, your manner and any favored very last results you may have for each of them. Simply realize which you are entire and you are enough and also you in no manner need any outside element to be entire. Detaching from people, situations, things and places is the maximum releasing enjoy of your existence. It does now not advocate, despite the fact that, that you forestall loving, no. It in reality technique that you are equipped to allow the whole thing move that now not resonates with you or serves you.

Free your self from the bags of your beyond.

Separation and what it truly approach

There is a commonplace false impression that originates from vintage, conditioned behaviour in regards in your past dating. The misconception is that separation for Twin Flames way the same as for a person else in a regular dating. I realise I made that mistake at the same time as we went into separation section and I panicked because I notion we have been breaking aside. Silly.

Let's positioned the time period Twin Flames aside, due to the truth we will study this in a broader term. The separation segment is your possibility to turn out to be entire without being dependant on any outside elements. Remember that at the identical time as you had been nevertheless in an unconscious relationship, you positioned conditions on the love you deliver and collect. You desired outside factors to your need to bloom. Your associate needed to be, appearance, say, count on, act like this or that.

Separation for a Twin Flame way to do the internal art work and end up complete. To stability your masculine and lady energy. To detach out of your companion and your dating. To cut the cords of co-dependancy.

TWIN FLAMES MASTERCLASS – Over 3.Five hours of examined equipment and first-rate insights with the beneficial aid of a real existence twin flame couple. CLICK HERE

To make it very easy: A separation section may be seen as becoming your right, effective Self. You apprehend that you do now not need everybody or some thing to present you like due to the fact you are unconditional love your self. And you recognize that, due to the fact you purchased again in your coronary coronary heart space.

Separation, as a technique to characteristic in your adventure to popularity, is the maximum profound segment you could likely undergo. Why? Because it's miles a cleaning of feelings, feelings, attachments and conditions.

The conditions you laid upon love for your past relationships do not hold up anymore. Being related to someone or a certain dating does now not serve you anymore because of the fact you recognize that you are one with everything and actually all of us. That you can and could do with out your partner.

Separation is coming at you to reflect upon your Self and do the inner art work. Stop complaining approximately how difficult it's miles. Stop whining approximately your partner no longer being conscious or wakeful. It is not approximately any outside element now. It is prepared your Self and the inner paintings to emerge as complete. And after you turn out to be whole, you have indifferent from any unique final outcomes. Will there be union? When will there be union? It doesn't rely quantity! Nothing subjects after you've got got efficiently mastered the separation section.

Remember that everything in lifestyles is available in cycles. You are being furnished the same opportunities to broaden (or in other words: disturbing conditions) over and over over again until you've got got mastered them one after the other. This lets in you to get to the subsequent degree.

Regardless whether or not you're man or woman, divine woman or masculine, you want to assemble and encompass every energies interior you. You can handiest end up entire thru balancing each energies interior you. Do not count on a few element to seem, or to your accomplice to do the provide you with the effects you need, and do no longer try to do the work to your associate both.

Separation manner to break up your Self from antique paradigms, situations, attachments, dependancies, behaviour, concept styles, to make room for some trouble larger and higher for your journey.

Chapter 13: The Magic of the Divine Feminine & Masculine

Written from a Divine Masculine attitude

Boys had been added up with the notion to suppress their very very own divine female power, or in exceptional phrases: their intuition, creativity, the float of things, love. Society has screwed up large time and one ought to ask the question if that end up designed intentionally.

The reality is that no guy will ever be complete without his Divine Feminine. That not simplest applies to the energies inside him, but also his Divine Feminine accomplice in life. This society is constructed upon the concept of separation and competition, as defined in our MASTERCLASS „An Awakened Man". This method that everyone's perception gadget is based totally definitely upon the idea that they'll be supposed to „make it by myself", to be higher than a person or have greater.

This belief device has been confirmed to be incorrect.

His Creation Powers

A guy, agency in his Divine Masculine and Divine Feminine energies, can assemble a few thing on this three-D worldwide with out competing with every body, because of the truth he's the creation pressure. He want to encompass every energies as a way to construct empires for him and his Divine Feminine companion. If his thoughts is rooted in opposition and separation, he will no longer emerge as whole indoors, and as a result in no manner acquire the quantity of popularity vital to collect his empire in three-D.

However, one thing ought to be said: A competitive mind can construct empires in 3-d as properly, however keep in mind that this journey can be paved with suffering and pain for himself, his own family and absolutely everyone worried. A man, rooted in opposition, will in no way create however as an possibility cast off from others, therefore making others undergo, therefore making himself go through. Nothing will ever be sufficient. He flourishes to have increasingly more. Notice that his goals are merely external elements, e.G. Extra coins, extra popularity, more interest.

Men who suppress their Divine Feminine energies are crippled in their ability to turn out to be whole, to truely live a lifestyles in abundance and to assemble their empire together with their Divine Feminine associate. They are chasing outside elements, which includes money, popularity, vehicles, houses, watches, luxury, and so forth. He has not located (however) to do the internal work, to get into his coronary coronary heart place and experience the unconditional love that he is and receives.

A guy, embracing both of his divine energies, is lots more effective than someone who's pushing through life with general unconsciousness. And but, he's privy to that he's, he in no way feels advanced, he in no manner receives back into competition mode. He is the advent stress for his Divine Feminine associate.

The Man and his Divine Feminine accomplice

For someone, and woman as well, it is critical to recognize and encompass each divine energies. There cannot be an architect (Divine Feminine) without the builder (Divine Masculine), no fashion dressmaker with out craftsman.

Coming together in a courting, even a Twin Flame Reunion, the manifestation powers of every companions merge into one normal strength residence. Both are balanced internal, knowledge their energies, and also data the dynamics in a aware courting as defined in the e-book Secrets to a Rich Relationship. There should be balance interior and balance on the out of doors. Whatever is to be created on the outside fact first ought to be created interior.

Energies

The combined forces of the Divine Feminine and Divine Masculine in a courting are able to tear aside their modern-day reality and create their preferred truth from scratch.

A man, being the Divine Masculine, need to thru all way embrace his Divine Feminine associate. He need to apprehend that he's the captain of their supply. And on the same time, he has to just accept the truth that he's absolutely the author for his Divine Feminine's creativity. He calls the pictures, builds their empire, effective, however without his accomplice he may not be able to create some issue of significance.

He has to remember his personal instinct, his Divine Feminine. Her connection to the universe is an lousy lot more potent than his private. He leads the manner, certain. And he in no way adjustments his mind virtually to pride his girl, certain. He has to guide her female because she is the sea for their supply, sure. He has to apprehend wherein goes (his purpose) and show the way, positive. BUT! Without being attentive to his Divine Feminine outside and inside, he gained't be transferring beforehand. Once recognize, this effective couple can create a few issue as their fact. They broaden in awareness, it definitely is the foundation and motive of their relationship.

The extra company a person is in his Divine Masculine energy, the greater his female accomplice can lighten up in her non-public Divine Feminine power. And vice versa! Remember that a dating primarily based absolutely absolutely upon the requirements of the three-d matrix is most probably to fail due to the truth the dynamics are wrong and misunderstood, the duties are combined-up, the power doesn't glide freely inside and thru the couple. Only by using the usage of knowing those objects is a aware courting feasible.

Purpose

Both are deeply rooted of their awareness. They recognize their purpose in lifestyles and both pursue it relentlessly. And considering anybody's motive is the identical – to feature to the development of humanity – they have a brilliant hazard to combine their forces under one flag, one challenge, one aim, one motive. A motive is what drives someone to construct empires. The gravity of his motive is pulling him beforehand effects. He is taking duty for his personal lifestyles, his options, his divine girl companion, his family, his industrial employer. As extended as he follows his motive. As lengthy as he acquired't permit all people distract him. Distractions are anywhere inside the three-D reality, however a person who is business enterprise in his energies and his reason can shrug them off with a smile.

Together as a pair, they're able to seem right away what it is that they want. It is all but a depend of surrendering to the established waft, obeying the general laws, setting intentions, and detaching from any unique final results. Remember that the universe is providing you with everything you need to create. Faith and receive as actual with in the normal advent powers is critical to stay in abundance and continuously be taken care of. The universe is great and could constantly offer you with abundance if you are open to receiving it.

Ascension Symptoms

Don't worry. Everything's gonna be okay

On your journey to ascension, end up the Divine Masculine and the Divine Feminine, you'll be confronted with severa adjustments interior your self and your frame.

When you have got correctly ignited the primary spark of interest, you may recognize small modifications within you. These modifications begin slowly and increase over the years.

It feels as despite the truth that your whole international is falling apart and being positioned once more together as a larger, higher and brighter fact. In the early stage of your adventure, these signs and symptoms and signs may be complex, or even scary. However, you need to now not worry the least bit because it's miles all a part of the bigger plan.

Change of Food

One of the most dramatic changes for your adventure is the meals. You have a take a look at that your antique conduct and weight loss plan does no longer serve you and your motive. You will maximum possibly wake up to the fact which you are one with the whole thing and absolutely everyone. You are one with the plants in addition to the animals.

You unexpectedly understand that an animal has the equal right to lifestyles than you do, and you can come to the conclusion that no animal can be harmed to your satisfaction.

As you development on your journey, you can feel that you are taking this even one step similarly. Going from vegetarian to vegan, or plant based totally weight loss plan absolutely.

In our workshop HOLISTIC LIFE DETOX, we display you the manner all meals is energy. And that the way animals are treated is going into their flesh, because of this, their fear of lack of life is being consumed through manner of you.

You in all likelihood received't be having this enlightening 2d very early on for your journey. It is a technique.

No greater (or little) processed food

As your recognition rises, you may experience how you're repelled with the aid of processed meals. Going through the aisles of a grocery store can also turn out to be like a horror film for you currently. You see the dairy branch, meat department, and you be conscious all of the useless animals wrapped up in plastic.

You see the being inside the again of the flesh and the manner it modified into treated inside the slaughterhouse.

I understand I maintain in thoughts how I felt when I stepped onto this stage of attention. I genuinely felt ill internal seeing the ones kinds of dead animals, the struggling, the ache, the death, properly wrapped up in plastic.

(If that makes your belly pull away, welcome for your awakening)

Organic, or bust!

Another critical alternate is which you are inquisitive about what's within the food and wherein it comes from. You will revel in the desire to buy natural tremendous due to the truth you want to recognize what you located into your body.

Change of Appetite

Your urge for food adjustments extensively. You revel in that you do no longer need as a good deal meals anymore, consequently, your frame weight changes substantially as well. And you won't even be aware it until you enjoy that all your clothes obtained't match anymore.

The quantity of food decreases significantly due to the reality you pay attention in your body more. You are not on a food plan, no. You truely have developed the plenty needed self-love via moving into your coronary heart region. This self-love permits you to like your Self and your body genuinely as they're.

Once you experience that unconditional love for yourself, your food regimen will exchange, your urge for meals will trade.

Sometimes, it would even feel awkward due to the fact you're craving various things now. Maybe a jar of mustard now appears so yummy that that is your dinner then. Do no longer fear. All is right. You in truth begin to concentrate in your body more carefully.

Chapter 14: Flu-like Symptoms

You can also moreover be conscious flu-like signs and symptoms every so often, e.G. Leap throat, fever, cold, fatigue, pain to your joints and your gums, and so on.

These are all symptoms and signs and symptoms and signs and symptoms that you are going upwards and ascend to better attention. Your frame, trapped inside the bodily three-D Matrix, is trying to seize up together together together with your 5D ascension. It almost looks like a plane flying through a storm: Scary, however you apprehend that it's far best quick. If you're a high-quality pilot ;).

Ascension symptoms, mainly flu-like signs, can seem very and also go away in no time. Before your first most crucial shift, there is probably a time even as you sense unwell for each week or maybe longer. Know that that is adequate. Listen on your body more cautiously now. Get rest. Drink enough water (watch the fluroid), and maintain a immoderate vibration.

Natural Sleep Rhythm

If you're in a feature in that you have got already withdrawn from the three-d Matrix paradigms of strolling 9-to-five, you can begin moving into your herbal sleep rhythm together along with your frame. Forget about no longer enough sleep, waking as masses as an alarm.

Once you are capable of absolutely allow your body take all of the sleep it desires, you may become with a higher health, due to the fact you are not forcing your body to move in opposition to its herbal rhythm.

If you haven't escaped the 3-D Matrix but, you will in all likelihood need to pay attention on your body and provide it the rest it dreams thru meditation or quick naps.

The traps of the matrix are very business enterprise. Getting up at a certain time, beginning work at a first-rate time, lunch destroy at a nice time. All of that is laborious on your frame as it is not the natural rhythm. And the device of the Matrix is designed to do simply that, to maintain you far from paying attention to your frame. That's why most human beings choose to concentrate to the TV at night time time in location of meditating. And bet what they consume via the TV: More pressure.

Change of Social Situation (Friends, Family, Inner Circle)

Let's face it: Not even circle of relatives contributors will apprehend your adventure. Even in case you attempt to provide an cause of it to them. The same applies for friends, your stylish network and your inner circle.

Your social community will considerably trade in case you actually give up to the regular float. You will feel that what your pals are speakme about does not resonate with you, and does now not fit your needs. Maybe they are into gossip, and that's some factor you wouldn't do (anymore).

No count number how tough it is, preserve in mind that human beings are getting into your life for a purpose, and in addition they go away your path for a cause as fast as you have observed your commands and are prepared to transport on.

No greater chit chat

As your reputation grows, you phrase that you now not want chit chat. You apprehend, this non-essential small talk stuff that you were taught to do to „be nice". Chit chat, together with climate, method, politics does now not resonate with you anymore. You pick to both speak approximately some issue massive that adjustments your life or the lives of others. Or stay in silence. Because in silence, there are extra answers than in terms.

How do we realize what desires to be healed?

Inner work, recuperation, clearing out past bullshit is an ongoing method for Twin Flames. Whenever Twin Flames are faced with what appears like a setback, it's miles simply the Universe telling you that you need to carry out a little more internal work.

Your Twin Flame is continuously a mirror of yourself. In an hassle, what hurts you'll be supplying you with a touch of what you want to paintings on. But on the equal time, what hurts you moreover mght hurts your Twin Flame, even if it's miles coming from them in an argument.

Consciousness and Awareness are crucial to your Twin Flame Journey, as is verbal exchange amongst your Twin Flame. There are instances of separation at the same time as you're supposed to be centered on your self for recovery and doing the internal art work. But Twin Flames who are in communique heal every distinct in a mystical manner. Even with arguing, there may be commonly the signal of restoration.

Opening as much as recognition technique to interrupt with all of your past belief tool, your ego, your feelings, your paradigms, your comfort zones, your existence. There isn't always something that doesn't need recuperation at the same time as the adventure starts, due to the fact every of you're coming out of an unconscious way of lifestyles.

How to do your Inner Work?

Becoming whole is one of the first things to do because of the fact on your heart location is in which you discover unconditional love for yourself. You will note how your ego will dissolve even as you begin loving your self unconditionally. Your paradigms will be clean to update. Your emotional reactions will dissolve and you invite increasingly more focus into your existence.

Letting bypass of any desired very last outcomes is the second one step, because of the reality you cannot even understand all the bliss and greatness of things that the Universe has in shop for you. Only your ego wants to cling onto a sure outcome. Let skip of that and invite abundance into your existence. Know which you are whole and also you do no longer want any outside component to experience love, no longer even some other character or companion. That is an important lesson to take a look at.

Surrender to what's. Do the whole thing you may, although, with what you have have been given. But if you have executed the entirety you can, certainly surrender to what's and to the tool. Know that you are continuously covered. However, do no longer expect that doing nothing is surrendering, no. Doing no longer whatever is ego. You ought to verify what it is that you may do in recent times with all of your might probable and passion, with what you have got to be had proper now. Only at the identical time as you probably did with a purpose to you invite benefits into your life.

A remarkable workout

One important workout for you to apprehend what needs to be healed is to transport returned home into your coronary coronary heart space. You are an infinite soul and your property in this physical body is your coronary coronary coronary heart area, in which your bodily coronary heart is located.

Through meditation, you could go away your thoughts space and detach from your horrible educate of thoughts, your feelings, your ego, your paradigms and notion machine.

In your coronary heart area, you can discover which you are unconditional love. You will discover your self-worth and yourself love. And this is vital to be able to end up your actual self.

When you are for your coronary coronary coronary heart location, you're very near who you without a doubt are. And you are capable of take a look at what it is which you need to art work on.

Overcoming the Obstacles of Reunion

Twin Flames are speculated to be together. Their adventure is past any over romanticised concept of a normal courting. They have come together in this lifetime to guide the world and bring recognition. And if you want to do this, they've got to triumph over their very own fears and insecurities. They should pass past their ego, their expectancies and their paradigms as a way to grow to be whole in my view and prepare for reunion.

A Twin Flame reunion is the natural flow of things. There isn't any resisting and no possibility. Twin Flames recognize that they'll be coming collectively in divine timing. When Reunion is close to, there may be an impossible to face up to pull, a gravity that is shifting every in advance, into togetherness.

The best hurdle every have to conquer that would put off their reunion is their very very personal selves. Nothing and no individual else can mess with Twin Flames. No out of doors element has any say of their adventure. Their relationship is quality navigated through their inner, truest Selves.

Twin Flames are their on compass, each emotionally and creatively in the three-d reality. They understand exactly what they have to do to turn out to be whole, they pull each one-of-a-kind forwards onto higher stages of increase and cognizance. They are one. They are union, and were lengthy earlier than they incarnated in this lifetime.

When the soul merges into the physical body, the soul slowly forgets about the information earlier than they incarnated. Earth is the soul's instructional playground. And the longer the soul is inside the frame, the extra it forgets about in which it first of all got here from.

This unlearning of the reality makes it possible for ego to develop, for paradigms to be shaped, for negative teach of mind to rise up.

This adventure right proper right here on earth, not most effective for Twin Flames, is one big cycle. You are presented the equal conditions time and again yet again until you have got observed out to grasp them. This journey is the equal for each soul incarnating in a bodily frame right proper right here on the planet.

For Twin Flames, their journey turns into instances as hard due to the truth now not high-quality do they need to stability their own energies inside, but moreover the energies between every notable on a miles deeper soul level than some other earthly relationship. Twin Flames are one soul in bodily our bodies. The soul has determined directly to incarnate like that because of the fact the collective now wishes a extraordinary shift in attention. And via nature, Twin Flames together are a effective pressure to ignite that shift, lead the shift, with the aid of instance, via sharing their expertise and experience.

The barriers for a Twin Flame reunion are continuously to be located in the Twins themselves. They should do the inner art work to crack their paradigms, move past their ego, get into their heart vicinity and be unconditional love. Without this art work, a reunion will now not arise because of the fact their religious boom in awareness and interest is mandatory for them to guide the collective shift.

When reunion is coming near, you may sense that tremendous pull, that gravity of your Twin Flame Union. Everything is taking area in hyper velocity. You simply need to permit go of any expectations, any pushing and insisting. When you're provided opportunities with the aid of the usage of the use of the universe, seize them. Say sure, even at the same time as you do now not apprehend the way to control it.

These possibilities are given to you through manner of the universe to rush up your union, because of the fact the actual strength of Twin Flames are unfolding while they will be collectively in union. They will create empires collectively, and they will be alleged to.

Do no longer permit your mind or ego trick you into wondering that this or that desires to be best in advance than union is viable. The Universe in itself is perfection enough to take your hand on this adventure and push you at the proper tracks. Do no longer forget your reunion by using way of manner of thinking you have to do more internal art work. You will experience whilst the time is proper. When it's time to let pass. Time to give up. Time to permit the beyond dissolve into nothingness without a doubt so your developing powers can materialise your new truth.

The Divine Masculine will take big movements as quickly as he has embraced his divine girl inside. He is aware of that he has this greater special instinct he can rely upon. And he desires to as a way to construct the empire for him and his Divine Feminine. The Divine Masculine has set his reason – the bodily reunion – and he is taking tremendous, perfect movement each day with what he has to materialise the reunion together along together with his divine female. He is aware the way to permit skip within the common float, knowing that the whole lot is coming in divine timing and in best divine manifestation.

Having carried out remarkable inner artwork, every Twin Flames are organized for reunion. Doubts approximately no longer being ready are traitors with the aid of the ego thoughts. These thoughts are best mind, based totally in fear, and haven't any energy over the Twin Flames, due to the truth they both are firmly in their coronary heart space, surrounded through unconditional love, self perception, self confidence and self love.

Surrender to the Gravity.

Chapter 15: Feeling unconditional love and detachment?

Yes, in reality. In truth, from my very personal revel in in my Twin Flame relationship, being indifferent is crucial for the Divine Feminine to emerge as privy to her very very own wholeness inside.

Detachment can act like a safety protect towards what's taking place for your Twin Flame relationship. Maybe topics are not going as expected. Being detached from any anticipated final outcomes way that you are whole regardless of what occurs.

It does no longer rely when you have union now or later or even in any respect. Being entire, giving and receiving unconditional love out of your coronary coronary heart area lets in you to live your life, artwork for your reason and experience each 2d of it.

Balance masculine & girl electricity for union?

Everyone has the Divine Masculine and Divine Feminine inner themselves. So it's far crucial to embody each essences with in you: The Mind (masculine) and the Heart (female).

When Twin Flames come collectively, they create a third entity, it is their relationship. Within that relationship, and this is vital now, each are available in with both more potent Divine Feminine or Divine Masculine.

So whilst every be part of in union, we've got a balanced Divine Masculine / Divine Feminine inside each considered one of them, and a balanced Divine Masculine / Divine Feminine interior their courting.

Sounds complicated, however genuinely it isn't.

I actually have connected a screenshot from our masterclass seminar

Screenshot_at_Mar_19_17_43_29.Png

Masculine ego pushing girl away?

Both, the runner and the chaser have the same internal artwork to do because of the reality that they are reflect of each other.

So if the Divine Masculine is pushing his Divine Feminine away, so is the Divine Feminine subconsciously.

They must crack & update their antique paradigms, pass past their ego, overwhelm their intellectual blocks to experience unconditional love for them selves first earlier than they're organized to dive into their Twin Flame courting.

If they may be trying to come together in advance, it does no longer paintings due to the reality there's still an excessive amount of unresolved, unconscious problems interior them.

Feel like crying after intimacy?

Speaking from a Masculine element of view, my Feminine desires to loosen up in my course. So I want at the manner to take the steering wheel and display the way in our relationship.

In order to do that, we needed to do loads of inner work first. Me constructing up my Divine Masculine, and she building up her Divine Feminine.

It seems like crying (in an awesome manner) due to the fact all of the partitions spherical our hearts crumbled down like crazy and we have been so inclined in each others hands.

We cracked & modified such quite some paradigms we had approximately self confidence, self-love, conditions on love, and so forth that it's far hilarious searching back at it now.

You moreover experience like crying because of the fact you can in the long run be your self, unconditionally. Your Twin isn't judging you, however loving you just the manner you're, with all of your strengths and weaknesses.

It took me some of hard internal paintings and struggling alongside my own non-public adventure, but it have become honestly nicely really worth each emotional outbreak and tear. I've placed the entirety collectively in this masterclass about An Awakened Man. Maybe it's useful for you too.

Can you forestall loving your dual at some point of separation?

The solution is not any. You love unconditionally so even inside the tough time of separation, love does now not dissolve or fade away. Separation section is virtually hard and there may be a constant push & pull, strolling & chasing, big confusion approximately your feelings and your Self. No count quantity how hard it gets, the love to your Twin Flame will in no way depart. You may moreover detach out of your Twin and from the final consequences, however you could in no way prevent loving your Twin Flame. Even at the same time as feelings are overflowing.

What does it propose to give up?

I turn out to be having a hard time accepting the concept of letting skip and surrender. I generally belief is manner to offer (a few factor) up. However, it is not. On the opportunity, it is making room for something large and higher than predicted.

Surrendering to what is technique which you acquire what's coming. You are not insisting on any anticipated or desired very last effects.

In regard on your query, it way which you take shipping of your Twin Flame connection and do not resist it or fight in opposition to it or push it to a quit end result you have in mind.

Now, it doesn't advise that you sit round looking for correct subjects to appear, no.

On my very very very own journey, I actually have positioned to stability my divine girl and divine masculine. Surrendering to what's and letting bypass of preferred outcomes takes place in my coronary coronary coronary heart location, my divine feminine.

However, even as you're to your Twin Flame adventure, there is a lot of hard work to do. In 3-d and inside your Self.

Activating and building up my divine masculine helped me to get topics performed, getting into the proper route, taking motion. When on the identical time my divine lady internal (coronary heart place) detached from and insisting on how the adventure goes to be, how prolonged, wherein, and so forth.

How do I love myself?

You want to constantly love yourself unconditionally, no longer best for your Twin Flame dating.

I had a tough time loving me unconditionally. I continuously needed outdoor gratifications or hobby to experience cherished. This modified into without a doubt stupid and overall unconsciousness. But additionally a brilliant getting to know for me.

I needed to waft out of my mind vicinity without a doubt and get once more home into my coronary heart space. It wasn't smooth due to the reality I needed to completely encompass my Divine Feminine internal and discover ways to permit circulate and give up. Quite a mission for me.

However, I felt masses love inner for my self and the entirety inside the Universe. I felt the unconditional presence of the universe. What an eye fixed consistent-opener!

To see that not anything within the 3d reality matrix definitely topics. Paying hire, paying payments, career, mission, residence,... this is all humbug and now not critical. What is vital is yourself-love, self properly actually worth, your being.

Cutting out Toxic People

You don't have time to waste on chitchat or gossip anymore. And even as you're an empath, you revel in the bad energies from folks that try this.

I did no longer reduce out such numerous human beings as hundreds as they simply disappeared from my adventure.

What I did changed into to emerge as whole, and this allows me to speak my inner reality with everyone: own family, ex, and plenty of others. Especially even as you are divorced with a toddler you want to turn out to be whole and talk your fact.

I remember on the equal time as my Twin Flame and I met, we did such plenty of factors that we wouldn't do anymore. Unconscious things like smoking cigars, ingesting meat, and so forth. We reduce that out too.

As you upward push in focus, humans will robotically go out of your manner when they cannot maintain up together together with your power.

I haven't felt the urge to get in contact with my antique buddies and connections. Unless it's miles a completely specific friendship. And I am first-rate with that.

Most humans received't understand. They want you to stay as that that they'd come to realise you. So what. It is your journey. More outstanding humans will be part of you on your way.

Blessings

PS: I choose no longer to talk if there is not something I can make a contribution from my inner truth. And I'm remarkable with that too.

Chapter 16: Why does my lifestyles enjoy like falling aside?

Your life HAS TO crumble to be able to remedy all that shit which you have been wearing with you your entire life.

If you took all the baggage with you, there is probably even extra suffering along the street.

The moderate you are asking for isn't on the prevent of the tunnel. The slight is inside you. You are doing such an superb paintings and you will be glad with you! The moderate, the solutions, the steering is to your heart space.

I experience that your ego continues to be a piece on the better element due to the fact ego desires you to hold within the consolation zones. Ego hates alternate. Ego hates whilst it's miles confirmed wrong.

You are doing the whole thing right while you're doing the inner paintings, crack your paradigms, bypass past your ego and flow once more domestic into your coronary heart location.

Trust the machine. The pleasure is in the journey, now not the holiday spot.

Let skip of expectations, be present inside the now, surrender to what's and grow to be complete.

Can I make my Twin Flame weight loss plan?

You can not make everybody carry out a little issue they don't want to. This is a way of awakening and a journey of interest.

From my non-public revel in, our eating habits and diets changed at exactly the identical time. Our journey might be very close to and similar.

When we met, we have been taking detail in our cigars, having a White Russian or Champagne sometimes, ingesting out at exquisite restaurants with meat, hen, and so forth.

But nearly on the same time we went vegan, stopped consuming alcohol (now not that we were alcoholics HAHA), stopped smoking cigars and changed our complete food regimen.

It modified into a totally intimate adventure because health is a sturdy bond.

Why all this self-assisting stuff?

The answer is simple: with out all this self-assisting stuff and keeping aside, there can be no together. Ever.

They ought to now not assist such hundreds of people whilst they'll be however entire of antique BS, paradigms, ego, conditional love.

This self-assisting stuff and the time aside is the journey to unconditional love, my luxurious. When this is completed, you may be capable of fulfil your cause together.

What are signs for the surrender of separation?

You can definitively sense the inner paintings that every of you have got have been given finished. That is essential to go back lower returned smooth collectively along side your past BS. What helped us have come to be to attention on our very own restoration turning into complete. We needed to detach from our expectation of the manner and at the same time as our reunion might occur. Everything takes area on the divine timing. Once you prevent the taking walks and chasing, and relax to focus to your Self, it does not rely whilst or how. You are entire and you feel unconditional love for your Twin.

What are regular schooling found for Twin Flames?

I'll describe my learnings from our Twin Flame courting, this means that that furthermore topics I positioned out approximately my Self. But given that we're TFs, she brought on those gadgets in me absolutely.

- Unconditional love

- Going past ego

- Cracking paradigms

- my lifestyles's purpose

- our soul challenge

- self assurance

- calmness

- empowerment

- compassion

- emotional expression

- embracing my divine feminine

- building up my divine masculine

- gaining knowledge of to permit pass, surrender and soar (freefall to the following segment in lifestyles)

- locating my internal reality

- coming once more to my coronary coronary heart area

- mind are stupid if not managed

- inspire human beings

- growing

- Detaching from anticipated effects

- How to grow to be a Power Couple collectively to construct empires

- Balancing my DM and DF

How do I conquer the concern of losing my Twin Flame

Get into yourHeart Space

In my heart area, I understood that I am unconditional love. I am whole and enough. The motive for a Twin Flame separation is to become whole simply so we're able to detach ourselves from our Twins.

Detach

Sounds much less complex said than accomplished. However, my Divine Feminine indifferent from me and he or she or he considered it as a safety defend closer to something will come. There is unconditional love amongst Twin Flames and not whatever will ever come between them. However, detaching is essential so you can allow bypass of any anticipated very last consequences and completely receive as genuine with the universe.

Trust the universe

Seriously, she is aware about what she's doing.

Enjoy the Ride

The method is more essential than the outcome. You'll studies so much about your Self, so in truth revel in it. If it's far your actual Twin then your fear of dropping is honestly created for your mind as a distraction.

You are not your thoughts

Fear lives to your mind vicinity. Thoughts of fear or losing a person is a give up quit end result of ego, out of doors factors, beyond critiques and no longer being for your coronary heart vicinity.

Know that you aren't your thoughts.

Chapter 17: How to Nurture Your Love for Happily Ever After

Once you have got were given located your Soul Mate, or the Twin Flame of your choice, you want to do extra than surely rely on your energy connections to look you via your journey collectively. It will high-quality ultimate an entire life if it's far a issue for each of you and is lovingly nourished each day of your lives. Here are a few beneficial guidelines winnowed from the understanding of many Soul Mate couples whose love and bonds preserve developing more potent and further attractive every year in their lives collectively.

1. Never save you courting

It is simple to allow the luster and exhilaration of a brand new relationship fade due to the reality the mundane workouts of life go through down upon you. However, lengthy-term a achievement love pals in no way appear to get out of the courtship mode. It can also tone down a

128

chunk as quickly as the connection is committed. But each partners but endure in thoughts to regularly do topics massive and small to offer themselves inside the incredible slight and permit their mate recognise by means of phrase and deed how a good deal they will be cherished and favored.

2. Consciously set apart wonderful time collectively each day

This will become specifically vital once you've got youngsters and pets. Their wants to it slow, plus artwork and what also can appear to be an ever growing listing of chores at home, can also go away little first-rate moments for every different in an afternoon. Don't allow it's so!

Find a time that works best for the two of you to have some tremendous by myself time despite the fact that it's miles simply to speak each day. Maybe within the morning even as you wake up, in advance than the each day rush begins offevolved, even it technique awakening a touch in advance to insure time for each distinctive. Evenings earlier than retiring are also a opportunity. However, thru the surrender of an prolonged day it is not uncommon for each to not be lively sufficient for high-quality time, mainly even as fatigue is calling you to clearly lay down and sleep. For some couples the outstanding time is quickly after they every get home from work. They make a factor of creating quiet moments collectively, to share a cup of wine or tea, to overlook the every day grind inside the peace of their home, inside the palms of the individual they love.

three. Understand and be OK with the fact that there can be bumps in the road

Things can nearly seem ideal in any new dating. That is mainly real for Soul Mates or Twin Flames. But actual lifestyles is not a fairy story. Even within the very excellent relationships, the stresses of existence get within the manner. How a pair offers with financial or health stressful situations, dating problems among themselves or of their extended family, work strain and busy existence traumatic schedules, will glide an extended way to figuring out the lengthy-term satisfying viability of their courting.

Successful couples understand and accept the truth that when every demanding challenge has exceeded, there may be another one to take its location in the long run inside the days to come lower back again. They are devoted to giving each one-of-a-kind one hundred% manual and peacefully and respectfully working out any variations that arise amongst them at the same time as presenting a united the the the front to any forces or people that would damage both one in each of them or their courting.

Rich or bad, everybody have challenges and although there may be some non violent respites, eventually new stresses arise and have to be handled. The exciting trouble approximately dating stresses is they will ruin vulnerable relationships, however will make sturdy relationships stronger. An apropos dating slant on an antique adage says, "Life is a grindstone. Whether it grinds your relationship down, or polishes it up, is based totally upon upon what it is fabricated from."

4. Be dedicated for your commitment

One of the tendencies that permits successful existence pals climate the storms of life, is that if they will be inclined to make the nice willpower to their accomplice, usually in the shape of marriage and a vow of fidelity. Thus joined, they emerge as decided no longer to barren region the supply in their dating regardless of how terrible the storms of lifestyles may also swirl. They comprehend that each one storms pass and last with their deliver is more secure and will supply them more achievement and prospects in the destiny than leaping by myself right right into a tiny lifeboat and jumping into the fury of the storm, hoping for the fine.

Of course, there are times even as one of the companions may additionally do an act so grievous that it scuttles the relationship deliver. It blasts a hollow so large in its hull that it could not stay afloat. That's a remarkable state of affairs, one that with a chunk of luck in no manner arises with Soul Mates or Twin Flames. For any lesser assignment, "united we stand, divided we fall," remains a bedrock truth.

5. Don't scuttle your supply of affection with the resource of appearing like an idiot

What are those idiotic form of actions that blow holes so huge your supply will sink regardless of the love or self-discipline of your accomplice? Adultery, little one abuse, alcoholism, drug dependancy and crook hobby of any sort, all screen entire disdain on your accomplice and your kids if you have any. They are usually bombs that blast holes that can't be repaired, so don't do them.

6. Date night time to stay proper

An rather useful a part of continuing the courtship technique is to make a dedicated concerted attempt to move on a date with the only which you love as quickly as each week. It can also just be an hour taking walks via the park, retaining palms and speakme. But it's also a top notch time to carry romance lower again that may be lacking at some stage within the moved speedy day cluttered with unique humans and obligations. This is one-on-one time to percentage embraces, hugs, kisses, adventures, explorations and rekindling the fires of affection, an extended manner from any and all regular distractions from kids, to paintings or chores.

Though as soon as per week is right, your every day existence may excellent permit multiple times a month. Make it some difficulty you may each count on and sit up straight for. Mark it on the calendar. Arrange for a babysitter. If you can't manage to pay for a babysitter, do a babysitting switch with buddies. One manner or some other, make it display up often and you can attain the rewards of a better, extra pleasant relationship every day.

7. Forgive and neglect, after responsibility common

Even in the super of relationships there can be times while your associate does a few issue that justifiably makes you truly dissatisfied. Not some thing as large as being untrue, however large sufficient that you could't help trying to yell at them.

If they were definitely responsible for a few factor that angered or damage you, they need to like you sufficient to confess their mistake, ask to your forgiveness and do what they could to make amends.

If they try this, you need to forgive them unconditionally, thank them for taking obligation for their mistake and repairing it in addition to they may. Then you want to in fact forget that it ever befell and show appreciation and love for your mate.

And clearly, to react with calm and acknowledgment of an mistakes is the movement of a person a ways extra enlightened than most. The natural response while someone starts offevolved offevolved expressing anger is to yell back at them in protection, even at the same time as you're within the incorrect. If your accomplice is higher than that and works to recovery their mistake, ensure you discard the anger and supply them love and appreciation for his or her efforts.

eight. Don't be a simmering pot

Sometimes in "for the connection," or "for the kids," one associate will go through in silence or close to silence on the same time as their mate says or does topics that hassle, offend or perhaps harm them. This isn't always a course that allows the connection or the children. Instead it regularly outcomes in a messy dating give up notwithstanding the reality that it can take some years down the road for it to upward push up.

Good conversation is actually as vital for Soul Mates and Twin Flames as it's far for everyone else in a romantic, lifestyles courting. It is wise to installation the addiction proper on the begin of a dating that encourages everybody to allow the alternative apprehend if a few component being stated or performed is affecting them negatively in any manner. Two human beings in love may also additionally have a scenario to carry out a bit thing they may to carry happiness to the opportunity. If the possibility is occurring, even unknowingly, as is frequently the case, talking approximately it early on washes away the power blockage which have end up building earlier than it has time to do any damage.

9. Two kisses a day keeps the divorce legal professional away

Of direction it is not quite that smooth. But small, tokens of affection, specially physical ones, given often while you are with every one-of-a-kind, which incorporates a kiss within the morning in advance than you detail techniques for the day and a kiss at night time earlier than you close up your eyes for sleep, supply each day reinforcement in your dating. Soft touches, eye contact, embraces and kisses confirm, "I love you, appreciate you, and am so thankful you're in my existence!"

10. Look for matters to praise

Giving reward to others, even a person you like deeply, doesn't come manifestly to everyone. Sometimes character or upbringing conspire to without a doubt no longer take into account it, or perhaps withhold reward. If that is the case, it is a terrible dependancy nicely well worth giving concerted attempt to interrupt, due to the reality sincere praise given with love, is a smooth, uplifting breeze that puts a buoyant wind of happiness into the sails of every person's deliver of lifestyles.

Og Mandino in his ebook The Greatest Salesman within the World, noted that we're all slaves to our behavior. But interior that reality, we will pick out to be a slave to nicely conduct, together with giving reward without issue and regularly, in place of the lousy dependancy of withholding it or making it conditional. Og furthermore referred to that you can't honestly prevent the awful addiction. You can simplest take away lousy conduct via changing them with right conduct. In this example, replacing withholding praise with seeking out things huge and small to regularly praise your associate and show gratitude and appreciation for. And there are overt praises which might be apparent kudos, and covert praises that though greater subtle nevertheless deliver a robust message of appreciation. Remember to best deliver sincere compliments. Words that could seem corny even as you take a look at them, become endearing and relationship strengthening at the equal time as spoken with love and sincerity to the only which you love.

Chapter 18: Need a few mind?

"I thank my lucky stars each day that I married you."

"You handled that state of affairs to perfection."

"You are this type of notable father/mom. I'm so satisfied you're the daddy/mom of our children."

"I love the way you likely did your hair in recent times."

"That have emerge as very innovative of you."

"You did a first-rate task on that project."

"That outfit appears clearly proper on you."

"I love the manner you smile."

"You're awesome. I'm so proud of you."

"I love you a lot. How did I ever get so lucky?"

"Thanks for supporting with that. It grow to be lots simpler with you."

"Wow! You did all that these days!"

"Thanks for looking after that chore."

"You are so clever."

"You have cute eyes. I love looking at them."

"Your smile melts my coronary heart as a remarkable deal these days because the first day we met."

"You are extra attractive to me than any of the stars in the movies."

"Being far from you is tough. I miss you."

"You are my fantastic pal. I'd as a substitute spend time with you than every body else."

"You have genuinely terrific taste."

"You are best for me absolutely the way you are."

"I'm so glad with you."

"You are in reality right dealing with human beings."

"I clearly respect the manner you may forgive and forget approximately and no longer maintain grudges."

"Being with you just feels so snug."

"You're remarkable!"

"Wow! You are looking better and better each day!"

"You're a genius!"

"Wow! Your dinner changed into like consuming at a connoisseur eating place."

"I like it while you do this."

"You are so smooth at the same time as you skip/stroll/dance/run."

"I must honestly use your advice on this."

"Your cool head got us through that."

"Thanks for being this form of difficult worker who typically does more than their percentage."

"You have a true interest in others that genuinely comes via. It's very admirable."

"You are so sexy."

"Your candor and honesty are very desired."

"Can you offer me your angle on this?"

"Sorry if I'm staring. You are like a beautiful piece of art work, I just can't take my eyes off of you."

"The finest blessing God ever gave me is you."

"It's fantastic how many guys/girls check you out as you walk with the resource of."

"You deliver the splendid neck rubs."

"I certainly appreciate you for _____."

"You are so funny now and again. I love that about you."

"I love taking note of your voice and speakme to you."

"Wow! You make those clothes look suitable."

"My pals are usually telling me how lucky I am to have you ever ever."

"My lifestyles is complete because of the fact you are in it."

"I in no way imagined a love as wonderful as yours for me and mine for you."

"You encourage me to be the tremendous I can be."

eleven. "When you have praise, shout it from the rooftop. When you have got were given criticism, chunk your tongue."

That become a announcing I heard every my dad and mom take me lower back to the fact of often as I end up growing up. It holds particularly real for couples which can be looking for a long-term, exciting relationship and is an vital element of Soul Mate and Twin Flame relationships. Praising your accomplice, letting them understand you recognize and recognize their excellence and efforts, especially in the the front of various humans, is a small motion that brings bountiful rewards. Criticizing your partner, mainly in the the front of different people, has exactly the other effect.

Sometimes complaint genuinely can't be held decrease lower back. Even in the ones conditions, examine the difference between optimistic and negative grievance and exercise giving extremely good criticism in a loving manner. The distinction is:

a) the terms you say,

b) your tone of voice and way of talking on the identical time as you say them,

c) and what phrases proceeded the criticism.

Make an extra attempt to maintain any criticism with reward, and appreciation creates a completely one of a kind prevent result.

Which of those examples would you respond to extra favorably?

"How generally do I even have to inform you to put the dishes in the dishwasher? I have requested you to do that a hundred times. Why do you never pay interest? What is so tough approximately rinsing a dish and putting it within the dishwasher? It takes all of ten seconds. You're making extra artwork for me and I'm uninterested in being your maid."

OR

"Honey, I love you a lot for all which you do. And I apprehend at the same time as you get domestic from work you're worn-out and truely want to eliminate doing some issue greater until all all yet again. I revel in that manner as soon as I come home from a difficult day at art work too. But neither humans sit up straight for having to address a pile of dirty dishes in the sink. I apprehend we've were given spoken approximately this in advance than and I don't need to be a nag, but that is some component this is vital to me. I without a doubt may apprehend it if you may absolutely take a similarly ten seconds to rinse your dirty dishes and placed them in the dishwasher. Can you please do that for me?"

With the exception of the few unusual people that enjoy arguing, anybody else might in reality pick the latter message delivery over the previous.

The first message might seem like an assault. The 2nd, like a pleasant, loving, respectful request. It may have loads better reception and opportunity of having the task finished as asked.

When attacked with criticism, each harshly or in a few times subtly, it can emotionally throw humans lower back to their early life when they have been scolded through parents, instructors or tremendous adults. This engenders emotions of anger, inadequacy, sadness, vulnerability and fear of outcomes.

Chapter 19: Criticism additionally produces considered one in all 3 outstanding reactions

a) Counter-assault

If you're being yelled at -- yell louder. Get computer virus-eyed, red inside the face and make your self so frightening which you cower your opponent and emerge as impervious to their assault. (I art work my tail off you SOB!) If you're being accused of inadequacy, hurl the alternative man or woman even larger faults yet again in their face. (Like how frequently have I knowledgeable you to close the rest room seat! And what about that big mess you certainly left within the lavatory? Is that a few issue else you sincerely expect me to take care of? You're the simplest that in no way listens and doesn't do enough to assist out!)

Counter assaults are a hundred% counter-effective. It turns love partners into adversaries, every looking for to win a war that alternatively every will lose.

b) Run Away

Many humans are considerably traumatized by way of the usage of manner of battle. When someone starts dumping on them with grievance, specifically if it is indignant complaint, their response is to escape the scene, which for the instant lets in dispose of them emotionally, in order that they don't sense guilt, afraid, disappointed, placed-downed or wronged. I've in fact visible people cowl their ears and run away. If the alternative man or woman is exploding in violent anger, leaving the scene can be the most steady and wisest preference in the mean time. But it can not be the identical vintage reaction to grievance. Avoiding the problem virtually frustrates the opposite character in addition and does not make the problem go away. It just makes it simmer. The hassle will stand up all yet again and due to the continuing unresolved simmer, the explosion will in all likelihood be even bigger than earlier than. Loving couples whose courting is crucial to them, recognize that smooth, respectful communication is an essential block inside the foundation of dating happiness and sturdiness.

c) Acquiesce

Sometimes you could offer too much searching for to thrill your associate. When one associate is criticizing the alternative and the individual being criticized fast acquiesces with, "you're right and I'm incorrect," they will be setting themselves up for even more criticism in the destiny because of the fact dominating them have become so smooth. More regularly than not, even as this is said it isn't due to the fact the person simply feels they had been being justifiably criticized, however certainly because they don't need to maintain in an difficulty. A festering resentment of their partner is generally the cease give up result.

Couples with robust bonds discover ways to art work thru frictions with love and mutual recognize by using manner of listening surely to the alternative man or woman, speaking softly now not harshly, and responding with praise in addition to critique or criticism.

Don't count on you're being useful with the useful resource of manner of being essential

The first question to invite yourself earlier than you say something critical is, "Is this something I want to say?" Unsolicited critique or complaint, at the same time as a person didn't ask on your opinion, is seldom preferred and nearly in no way desired.

Some human beings boom a terrible dependancy to critique or criticize others, justifying their actions through manner of manner of wondering they may be sincerely assisting them thru mentioning their faults or shortcomings. However, maximum human beings are very privy to their faults and shortcomings and don't want surely everybody to element them out, unless they have got mainly requested for their opinion and positive criticism. For instance, telling your buddy, accomplice or member of the family that they have to possibly shed kilos for the sake in their fitness is a diffused grievance, notwithstanding the truth that it may be real. It isn't always a few thing they may be not already privy to. By pointing it out you're genuinely reminding them that they're overweight and making them experience undesirable.

12. Don't keep rating

A positive way to constantly locate your relationship lacking is to preserve a intellectual score about how a whole lot you are doing in comparison to how an entire lot your partner is doing. This will usually frame your courting in negativity. It can run the gamut from who contributes more financially, to who does extra chores, to who expresses like to a greater amount, to who's extra responsible, to who does extra to hold own family solidarity and harmony and on and on and on. If you need your courting to very last and thrive you clearly can't try this – the least bit!

In a wholesome dating with reciprocity, there may be no basis for retaining rating. Both companions will continuously be recommended from love and devotions to do all they're capable of, each in their personal manner, to make a contribution to the health and happiness of the relationship and own family. And everybody will understand, appreciate and widely known the efforts of their companion.

If you're in a courting in which it's miles hard not to keep rating because of the reality there may be this type of yawning hollow among your efforts and paintings in contrast to your partner's contributions, the inequality factors to deeper troubles. If you figure a technique then come home tired, to piles of chores, at the same time as your associate sits round, eating beer, searching TV, thinking even as dinner can be prepared and the laundry finished -- unluckily, that normally stems from an entire existence of bad behavior which might be maximum now not going to exchange specifically inside the event that they didn't exchange at the inception of the connection, the time your partner desired to pride you the maximum. In the ones instances, love yourself sufficient to now not be a martyr. You deserve higher and better is offered looking for you.

In in search of your Soul Mate or Twin Flame you can find out a person who is continually looking for processes to make your courting better and more pleasurable for you. They derive top notch pride from seeing you glad. As every human beings see their life collectively through the equal window of the others happiness, each in fact grow to be doing all they may be capable of to make it so.

thirteen. Dedicate the primary yr to every one-of-a-kind

This is not as essential for couples who've carefully seemed every splendid for years. But for definitely absolutely everyone else, a honestly treasured block in the dating basis is laid down whilst a couple dedicates their first three hundred and sixty five days of married life to spending as a whole lot time as viable with every specific. Lifetime conduct of love, information, devotion and desire to deliver a smile and happiness to the opposite are created inner this cocoon of precise time collectively.

If viable, avoid pressure inducers and time gulpers collectively with: an intense university curriculum, a excessive-pressure hour-eating pastime, beginning a ultra-current business enterprise business enterprise, and even being pregnant. Create as masses time for each great and as little time for sincerely every person and the entirety else, and you may forge an top notch bond and be remembering and thanking yourselves for making that desire every 12 months of your lives together.

14. Couples that play together live collectively

Having energetic enjoyment and undertaking hobbies that you may revel in together with a laugh and laughter, with out getting riled up in competitive sports activities, is a in particular valuable couples bonding tool.

Though all of us will likely nonetheless have pursuits, enjoyment and task options that their partner has little hobby in, frequently sharing ones they do each experience is a love unifier. It can be whatever from gambling gambling cards or board video video games, to hikes, to racket sports activities activities sports activities, or stay indicates where they admire the identical tune. The primary substances are a stage of energetic participation and that it's miles a few element precise, now not an regular prevalence. For those motives it does not embody passively sitting collectively looking tv suggests, which creates very little interplay and is adequately mind-numbing in that many humans can't even keep in mind the plot of indicates they watched the preceding night time.

Though they are less passive than trekking or racket sports activities activities sports, live shows and theater movies or plays are nonetheless dynamic joint leisure because of the reality they're set apart as particular dates, with particular shared pleasure inside the entertainment. Plus, as set apart dates a live performance, theater film or play will probably be loved sitting carefully issue-through-factor, preserving arms and proceeded or discovered through a romantic dinner date.

15. Spice existence with spontaneity and surprise

This is going nicely with remembering the little matters. Some humans claim they don't like spontaneity or marvel and that's exquisite. That simply is some peoples individual – up to a point. What they normally actually advocate is that they don't like having their planned schedule disrupted. This trait has a tendency to get extra stated as people age. No trouble, just art work your marvel or deliberate spontaneity into their time table. Let them understand they want to dam out fantastic hours for a wonder you have were given planned. That little trick will insure they'll be looking ahead with interest to the marvel in place of being upset with having their agenda disrupted. Even spontaneity may be deliberate. Again, just ask them to dam out some time for you on a day at the same time as you each have no one-of-a-kind plans. Once a while arrives, begin thinking about what you will do -- truely spontaneous internal a deliberate time body!

16. Remember the little topics – regular.

The occasional huge gives and tokens of loving sentiment are extremely good, however it is the normal little acts of affection and appreciation that depend the most. A short-term loving contact; a warmth smile; a sweet endearment whispered within the ear; doing all your aspect for chores across the residence; a surprise hug from in the back of; an extended, loving gaze; attaining out and preserving arms while walking; usually talking respectfully; wonder cleansing and washing of their automobile; a hand located softly to your partners thigh whilst you sit down, remembering to mention thank you and show gratitude; the ones are some of the little jewels of affection, well worth greater than gold.

In addition to moderate touches and unexpected expressions of love and appreciation, right here are some mind for little matters that suggest plenty! Most of them have the first-class effect if they'll be carried out all at once and no longer for a commonplace particular occasion like a birthday, anniversary or Valentine's Day.

a) Give your lover a foot rub even as you're sitting together at the couch searching a show. Inevitably it's going to alternate proper into a mutual foot rub, so that you get as a first-rate deal as you give!

b) Leave quick written notes in sudden locations. "I love you!" "You're the greatest!" "You're my dream come authentic!" "I can't get hold of as real with how lucky I am to have you ever as my spouse/husband." "I'll have something particular for you whilst you get domestic this night." Place your notes in locations you already know they'll find out them as a wonder in the course of the day. Some proper spots include, inner their eye glasses case, on the steerage wheel of their car, interior a cupboard they open each day, on their hand reflect, on their shaving razor, in their coat pocket, changing the bookmark in the e-book they may be analyzing, inside their lunch bag, an email on their pc, or a show screen saver!

c) Say thanks. Simply giving sincere thank you, specifically for small efforts, is pretty a warming balm to the coronary coronary coronary heart and increases the bonds of love.

d) Mail a card of love for no event. Don't watch for a birthday, anniversary or Valentine's Day. Send him/her a unique card in that you for my part write about your affections and appreciation. Because it isn't for a selected event it may propose a fantastic deal greater. You are predicted to remember the only that you love on ordinary vacations. When you display you're considering them on other days, it's miles an affidavit to the depth of your affection.

e) Send her/him a card or e mail with something humorous. This is mainly powerful if you can relate it to some thing humorous the two of you expert collectively. People do not forget times they laughed together approximately some trouble they were experiencing. For instance, a card with a photo of a small dock going out proper right into a placid lake. Hand written internal, "This reminded me of the time I jumped in the lake and pulled you in with me."

f) Compliment them about the manner they appearance, their garments, how they scent, the manner their new hair cut makes them look extra younger or greater stunning or virile.

g) Make them breakfast in bed. Always a top notch romantic way to reveal you love and recognize your companion. It works quality at the same time as it is carried out spontaneously and not for a specific event.

h) Do a venture they hate for them and permit or no longer it's far a wonder discovery. When someone is dreading doing a chore they need to do after which to their pride find out their lover has finished it for them, it lights pretty some fires of affection.

i) Lighten their temper with tune. On a day whilst you get home in advance than your companion, put on their desired music. Their mood and mind of you will be buoyed from the instant they circulate the edge. Music, if it is a kind that a person resonates with, touches their soul. If you are the only that made it feasible, so do you.

j) Watch the video or have a check the images of your marriage and early years together. Often times a walk down memory lane reminds every of you of why you obtain collectively inside the first place and brings up satisfied memories from the beyond. Looking lower back on all of the applicable times you've shared is a reminder of techniques specific your dating is; some difficulty that might occasionally be forgotten inside the hustle and bustle and annoying situations of existence.

ok) Do it- ultimately! There is constantly some aspect your accomplice has asked you to do which you have ignored looking after: a person to call, an appointment looking to be set; taking a pile of vintage clothes to the second hand keep; cleaning out the closet or the shed.

l) The opposite neck kiss & hug. Guaranteed to let her or him understand you adore and appreciate them with out pronouncing a word! Without scaring them, rise up behind your accomplice, located your arms round their waist and nuzzle their neck, then kiss them softly in multiple places along their neck and in the back of the erogenous area of their ear. It could be a sign of love they may no longer neglect approximately, however will flip and reciprocate with a heat coronary coronary heart. If you're a short female and want to do this on the aspect of your guy, wait until they'll be seated in a chair you may effortlessly upward thrust up inside the back of.

m) Text or sext your lover messages in some unspecified time within the future of the day. From harmless thoughts of affection like, "I'm considering you and your huge blue eyes," to erotic pics or texts. Send them some component each hour and they'll want to go back domestic early in their exhilaration to be with you.

n) Spontaneously exit to devour on a night time time on the identical time as one or every of you return domestic tired from art work. If neither has to prepare dinner or easy up the kitchen, a venture that turn out to be likely being dreaded, it makes the tiring day be nearly surely forgotten. As a further love enhance, whilst the state of affairs arises and your companion doesn't just like the meal they ordered, switch plates with them and offer them yours or percentage every together.

o) Offer to assist. Each character normally gets into the dependancy of doing sure chores -- his chores and her chores. Unexpectedly coming and helping your accomplice with chores they had been anticipating to need to do on their very own, will continuously carry a grin of appreciation and in the future lots extra!

p) Give a foot bath and rub. Let them sit down down once more and watch their favored film or display on the equal time as you stick their tired bare ft in a basin of warmth (however now not too heat) water with Epsom Salts you've organized. After the water starts offevolved to relax offer them a foot massage to finish off the marvel.

q). Give them a candle-lit bathtub and towel rub. Prepare a heat bathtub for them and moderate the room with candles or LED candles, put on their desired music and perfume the water with their desired critical oil. When they come out provide them a energetic towel rub over each a part of their frame to dry them off.

r) Make a thriller pampering appointment for them, however now not for a completely unique occasion. Find a few issue you realize they will certainly love like a professional rubdown or a nail cutting. Tell them you've got got a wonder for them and they need to set aside a effective time. Pick them up and allow it is a marvel in which you are taking them.

s) Slave for an afternoon. This may be real amusing for both of you. The primary premise is to really serve and pamper them in each way. Make all their food, deliver them their beverages, open doorways for them, prepare their bathtub, within the event that they need a few component you get up and get it. If you want to carry the undertaking into the bed room, it could add quite the spice to intimacy.

t) Public kiss is a can't miss. Showing your affection with a kiss in public, the extra human beings that see it the higher, indicates your companion you're proud to like them and no longer bashful to permit each person apprehend.

u) Play video video games together. Great for a wet weekend day. Get out your preferred board video games, card games, or Ninetendo Wii undertaking. Relax and feature a laugh together with out getting too competitive. Later inside the nighttime there is probably a few mattress room video games you make a decision upon over parlor video video games.

v) Lover's nickname and terms of endearment. Having someone you want call you with the aid of a pet call truly makes you experience special. The call itself seems unimportant. In France, I've heard human beings name their lover "mon grand can" (my massive duck) and "mon petit chou" (my little cabbage). In America I've heard people call their accomplice "peanut," "burp" "go through" and "vintage shoe." Those thrilling terms of endearment seem to soften hearts and convey smiles however the much less than flattering terms. So the impact is manifestly in appreciation for having a completely unique nickname or endearment and not always in what the phrases are simply depicting. Similarly, terms of endearment like "honey," "sweetie," "darl'in," "sweetheart," "love," "lover," and "babe," want for use frequently in area in their given name, setting you and your affections for them apart and above honestly every person else.

w) Hold arms, take a seat down close to, never lose your more youthful love. Touch is an outstanding conveyer of affection and affection. If you've ever checked out vintage married couples, those which have been together for more than three a long time, you'll now and again see couples who act like they'll be though newlyweds. They commonly sit down next to each different, despite the reality that stroll down the road retaining arms, and while you be aware them test out each different's eyes you may't preference but have a observe the sparkling appearance of affection they share with each unique. Being capable of particular their love so sincerely after such hundreds of years, didn't certainly take place to them. You understand it's far some factor they've got worked at and made a priority for all in their lives collectively. A right lesson for all of us.

x) Run your palms via their hair and lightly run your fingernails over their scalp for a couple of minutes genuinely as they lay all of the way proper right down to doze off. This is fantastically fun and warmly endearing and preferred.

y) Late night time treats. Make an excuse to go to the store for some thing multiple hours earlier than mattress and are available home along side your fans preferred dessert.

z) Don't be hesitant to mention "I'm sorry," whilst it's miles suitable. Being willing to confess fault if you have truly made an mistakes is a difference of a higher being and a trait of sturdy couples.

All relationships take self-discipline and effort to help them final through the years and get past life annoying situations nevertheless united. You can't neglect to reveal your love each day in small strategies. A love courting is much like the most lovable of all plant life, with an captivating perfume that is intoxicating and a wonder that enraptures. But for it to stay all the time in all its glory, like each touchy flower it must be nurtured cautiously and constantly.

Twin Flames and Soul Mates begin with the advantage of getting greater harmonious strength connections and not unusual interests and desires than run-of-the-mill relationships. But in that greater enhance do not turn out to be complacent. All relationships that final, persevering with to help each person increase and increase and into the crescendo in their ability and success of their happiness, achieve this handiest due to the truth that have become the goal from the very first day and the try made each day in their lives together to make it so.

May you find out and love your Soul Mate thru all your days of existence and past. It is the high-quality success you may ever apprehend -- in case you make it so.

Chapter 20: Beware of the wolf in sheep's clothing

One of the most vital desires in existence that many human beings have is to fulfill their dual flame or their soulmate. It is regularly tough to tell whether you've got got honestly met yours. There are wolves in sheep's apparel near relationship. There are psychopaths, sociopaths, predators, bullies and toxic human beings in preferred which you need to keep away from while you are trying to meet the man or woman of your goals.

You will have to kiss a whole lot of frogs earlier than you find out your prince. Personally, I dated plenty in advance than I met my prince. It took me an extended amount of time to figure out what I desired in a accomplice, what may additionally want to paintings for my lifestyle, and what signs and symptoms and symptoms to look for to decide at the identical time as a relationship changed into poisonous. People stay in relationships a first-rate deal longer than they should, and masses of these relationships motive things like complicated PTSD from relationship abuse and trauma. Sometimes, each people inside the courting experience abused. They each component the blame at every other even as the truth is that they'll be like oil and water inside the dating.

If you're pretty or confident or a achievement in live, you may likely have a whole lot of suitors lining as lots as take you out. Many of them are in search of to get with you for the wrong reasons. You will find that a whole lot of them nice need your cash, sex or property. A parasitic and toxic character receives with you due to the truth she or he goals an area to stay or a person to feed her or him. A character may additionally get with you so you can open new opportunities for them at work, or they may date you to meet their own family nagging them to get married and function youngsters.

Getting into the incorrect dating can literally get you murdered. If your companion isn't in reality in love with you, she or he ought to cheat. His or her lover need to decide ultimately that they need you out of the image. Even the sweetest, maximum harmless humans are able to murder if the conditions are right. Don't ever be within the center of a love triangle. If you discover yourself competing with someone else to your accomplice's affections, you are in the incorrect relationship.

This e-book will assist you to determine brief whether or no longer you've got had been given absolutely met your soulmate, or whether or no longer or now not you are losing a while with an not feasible imposter a excellent way to never pan out into a totally practical courting.

How does a dual flame range from a soulmate?

Soulmates are stated to be suits, at the same time as dual flames are mirrors of every different. You may revel in as even though the 2 of you're twins on many stages. You also can find which you have the identical desires, interests, existence motive, values and morals. You can also moreover have professional maximum of the identical existence memories, even terrible studies like toddler abuse to your young people.

You can also have suffered from comparable traumas at some point of your existence. You also can every were divorced or out of place a child. You can also have each been in vehicle injuries. You may additionally have each accompanied the same shape of personal development or career improvement. You might also moreover each have the same art work ethic. Whatever the similarities, you enjoy like you're looking at yourself in a replicate. Your twin flame looks as if he or she is much like your self, and also you get to realize them lots faster due to the fact you revel in like they may be your reflect.

What are the symptoms I even have met my dual flame?

1.   Your dual flame may want to have a feeling of familiarity. You will experience just like the 2 of you've got were given met before. You may moreover have simply met in advance than in a past existence, or the two of you may have dated other people whose portions and additives remind you of your twin flame.

2.   Your twin flame will encourage your personal growth. You gained't experience like your twin flame is sucking the life out of you. On the opposite, you could experience complete of existence collectively along with your twin flame. You will energize every different, and the two of you may

need to spend masses of time together. You offer plenty-wanted assist to every extraordinary, and you turn within the direction of operating for your shared dreams collectively after you meet due to the reality you experience comfortable doing so.

3.   You don't fear continuously that your dual flame will leave you. Your dual flame will look at your signs of lack of confidence, and he or she or he can be capable of reassure you before you ever ask to be reassured. You obtained't enjoy tension within the pit of your stomach due to the truth your other half of continuously places you on element and makes you doubt the relationship. That's no longer to say that you won't have fights sometimes. Every couple ought to workout their variations, and the twin flame fights will lead them to more potent than ever in advance than.

4.   The dual flames complement every other. Whatever you aren't right at, your

twin flame can be excellent at. Whatever regions your twin flame is weak in, you could fill within the hollow. The of you fit collectively like a glove. You will each be able to have a observe matters from opposing views, but you can assist every different develop via way of manner of making the other see topics openly and virtually.

five.   You obtained't be afraid to reveal or percent topics collectively with your dual flame, due to the fact they will in no way use the facts in the direction of you or to damage you want distinct poisonous humans may additionally. You will revel in comfortable with them, and you will enjoy cushty being there for them. You received't feel like you're continuously losing time together along with your twin flame for your courting due to the truth the 2 of you can all the time be constructing something tremendous.

6.   Your twin flame will show display all the nicely and horrible factors of you. The of you would possibly proportion a number of the identical topics that you each have to art work on. When you work on the ones private increase regions together, it's miles now and again notably painful. You will feel prone and uncooked, however you will additionally sense like you can face those areas of your existence at the aspect of your twin flame via your side. You may be able to have a look at the darkish aspect of your twin flame with out being afraid, and your dual flame can be amazingly accepting of your flaws.

7.   You should have raw and unadulterated conversation together along with your twin flame that you can't have with extraordinary humans. Your twin flame will name you out on subjects even as you're being a jerk, and you won't be afraid to mention a few issue on your twin flame about their flaws. The of you recognize

that, even if you proportion tough conversations, you continue to ultimately love and assist every distinct.

eight.   You will lose manipulate of yourself even as you're collectively together with your dual flame. You will leave out them intensely at the same time as you are a long way from them. You will face feelings which you haven't needed to deal with earlier than. Your twin flame attracts out all the factors of you which have been hidden away and suppressed all of your lifestyles. This happens in a non-abusive way. If you enjoy abused through the usage of the usage of someone, this is not a sign of a dual flame. Some people mistake narcissistic and poisonous relationships for dual flame unions. The twin flame union hurts, however in appropriate methods that help you to amplify — they don't suppress and batter you into dread, hopelessness and despair.

9.   You normally have each other's backs. Your twin flame will take your trouble numerous the time, even while you're incorrect. The of you may be inclined to get arrested collectively if it is for a super motive. You will propose as a united front toward the sector at the troubles every of you sense strongly for or in the direction of. You will sense like you have a associate in crime. Other humans may be jealous that you have a integrated twin to assist you via some factor you could enjoy in life.

10. You will download books like this and wonder whether or not or not that is surely 'the only'. You might not accept as proper with that your desires have come to fruition. You can also additionally split along with your dual flame due to the truth you are afraid to take the connection to the following degree.